"In this innovative and wide-reaching work, Eleonora Viganò presents a new theory of how people think about and interact with their future selves. Far from a simple matter of self-control, Viganò shows us how our intertemporal trade-offs have a potent moral dimension. This book inspires a new view of selfhood and has considerable implications for the way we act in the present with our future in mind."

—**Adam Bulley**, *Harvard University and the University of Sydney*

Moral Choices for Our Future Selves

This book investigates the relationship between our present and future selves. It focuses specifically on diachronic self-regarding decisions: choices involving our earlier and later selves, in which the earlier self makes a decision for the later self.

The author connects the scientific understanding of the neurobehavioral processes at the core of individuals' perceptions of their future selves with the philosophical reflection on individuals' moral relationship with their future selves. She delineates a descriptive theory of the perception of the future self that is based on empirical evidence and that systematizes and integrates the current theoretical literature. She then argues for the morality of prudence and interprets diachronic self-regarding decisions as decisions between two agents—the earlier and later selves—that belong to the realm of intergenerational ethics, which regulates the relationship between contemporary people and future generations. Finally, the author provides a moral theory of prudence based on respect for one's agency. This theory identifies what the present and the future selves owe to one another in diachronic self-regarding decisions.

Moral Choices for Our Future Selves will be of interest to scholars and students working in ethics, moral psychology, philosophy of mind, and cognitive science.

Eleonora Viganò is a Postdoctoral Researcher at the Institute of Biomedical Ethics and History of Medicine at the University of Zurich, Switzerland. Her work focuses on self-regarding morality, the neuroscience of ethics, and digital ethics.

Routledge Focus on Philosophy

Routledge Focus on Philosophy is an exciting and innovative new series, capturing and disseminating some of the best and most exciting new research in philosophy in short book form. Peer reviewed and at a maximum of fifty thousand words shorter than the typical research monograph, *Routledge Focus on Philosophy* titles are available in both ebook and print on demand format. Tackling big topics in a digestible format the series opens up important philosophical research for a wider audience, and as such is invaluable reading for the scholar, researcher and student seeking to keep their finger on the pulse of the discipline. The series also reflects the growing interdisciplinarity within philosophy and will be of interest to those in related disciplines across the humanities and social sciences.

Confucianism and the Philosophy of Well-Being
Richard Kim

The Repugnant Conclusion
A Philosophical Inquiry
Christopher Cowie

Totalitarianism and Philosophy
Alan Haworth

Moral Choices for Our Future Selves
An Empirical Theory of Prudential Perception and a Moral Theory of Prudence
Eleonora Viganò

For more information about this series, please visit: www.routledge.com/Routledge-Focus-on-Philosophy/book-series/RFP

Moral Choices for Our Future Selves

An Empirical Theory of Prudential Perception and a Moral Theory of Prudence

Eleonora Viganò

NEW YORK AND LONDON

First published 2023
by Routledge
605 Third Avenue, New York, NY 10158

and by Routledge
4 Park Square, Milton Park, Abingdon, Oxon, OX14 4RN

Routledge is an imprint of the Taylor & Francis Group, an informa business

© 2023 Eleonora Viganò

The right of Eleonora Viganò to be identified as author of this work has been asserted in accordance with sections 77 and 78 of the Copyright, Designs and Patents Act 1988.

With the exception of Chapter 3, no part of this book may be reprinted or reproduced or utilised in any form or by any electronic, mechanical, or other means, now known or hereafter invented, including photocopying and recording, or in any information storage or retrieval system, without permission in writing from the publishers.

Chapter 3 of this book is available for free in PDF format as Open Access from the individual product page at www.routledge.com. It has been made available under a Creative Commons Attribution-Non Commercial-No Derivatives 4.0 license.

Trademark notice: Product or corporate names may be trademarks or registered trademarks, and are used only for identification and explanation without intent to infringe.

Library of Congress Cataloging-in-Publication Data
A catalog record for this book has been requested

ISBN: 978-0-367-63493-3 (hbk)
ISBN: 978-0-367-64095-8 (pbk)
ISBN: 978-1-003-12214-2 (ebk)

DOI: 10.4324/9781003122142

Typeset in Times New Roman
by Apex CoVantage, LLC

For Belle Donino

Contents

Funding		x
Epigraph		xi
Acknowledgments		xii
	Introduction	1
1	How do we perceive our future selves? The neurobehavioral basis of one's perception of the future self	8
2	What is the nature of the relationship in which we stand with our future selves? Practical and moral issues of one's perception of the future self	38
3	How should we treat our future selves? The moral requirements of prudence to one's present and future selves	60
4	How does the Moral Theory of Prudence work in practice? The application of the theory to advance healthcare directives in dementia	93
	Conclusion	114
	Index	118

Funding

This work was supported by the Cogito Foundation (Grant 17–117-S).

Epigraph

We are the outcomes as well as the makers of our choices.
—David Schmidtz ("Self-interest: What's in it for Me?", 1997: cit., 109)

We do, in fact, need a theory of intra-personal justice specifying what one owes to oneself, and from which perspectives one owes it.
—Paul Schofield ("On the Existence of Duties to the Self (and Their Significance for Moral Philosophy)" 2015: cit., 527)

Acknowledgments

Even before studying philosophy, the relationship in which we stand with ourselves caught my attention, and reflecting on it has been part of my attempts to live well and to get the most out of my life. As a philosopher, I began thinking about the moral relationship with oneself at the end of my PhD at the Faculty of Philosophy at Vita-Salute San Raffaele University in Milan. I am grateful to my professors and colleagues there for inspiring discussions on the topic—in particular, Roberto Mordacci, Massimo Reichlin, Roberta Sala, Francesca Pongiglione, and Sarah Songhorian.

I worked on a project regarding the empirical and philosophical understanding of our relationships with our future selves at the Institute of Biomedical Ethics and History of Medicine (IBME), at the University of Zurich. That project is the base of this book and was funded by a scholarship from the Cogito Foundation. I would like to thank that foundation—and, in particular, Irene Aegerter—for supporting the research on which this book is based and for giving me the opportunity to work at the IBME. I have been fortunate to be part of this institution, and I am grateful to my colleagues for the stimulating conversations I had with them regarding several ideas in this book.

I owe a debt of gratitude to Markus Christen for supervising and believing in my project on the understanding of our relationships with our future selves. He gave me helpful suggestions on the first part of this book and fundamental advice about my academic career.

I am deeply indebted to Michele Loi for reading and extensively commenting on much of the book and for encouraging me in carrying out my proposal. His incisive criticism has been as invaluable as his understanding of the challenge that I faced in writing a book while completing two other projects, one of which was led by him.

I am thankful to Philippe Tobler, Daniel Bartels, an anonymous reviewer at *Cognitive Science*, and another anonymous reviewer at *Philosophical*

Psychology for their valuable comments on an early draft of the first chapter. I am grateful to Sebastian Wäscher for the stimulating discussions of the two central chapters of my book and to Elena Tagliabue for providing me with her medical expertise regarding the last chapter.

I owe great thanks to Marcus Arvan for his very helpful feedback on the book—and, in particular, on my Moral Theory of Prudence. I would like to thank an anonymous reviewer at Routledge for their suggestions on the book proposal, the editor Andrew Weckenmann for his enthusiastic interest in the book, as well as the editorial board and staff at Routledge.

I benefited from presenting and discussing parts of my Moral Theory of Prudence (developed in Chapter 3) and its application (discussed in Chapter 4) at the tenth European Congress of Analytic Philosophy (ECAP 10), the 2020 Research Colloquium on Biomedical Ethics of the IBME, and the XI Braga Meetings on Ethics and Political Philosophy.

Introduction

On various occasions throughout life, we doubt whether, in the past, we made the best choice for our present selves, or we do not know at present what is best for our future selves. Sooner or later, everyone will face a decision that gives rise to such thoughts—for instance, the choice between dedicating oneself to a job career and having a family, when the two options cannot be reconciled in one life. Another example is choosing to move to another country, an unfamiliar environment with more life opportunities, versus remaining in one's home country, a familiar environment with fewer life opportunities. Such choices are termed *diachronic self-regarding decisions*. They are *self-regarding* because they involve the individual making the decision and her relationship with herself. They are *diachronic* because they involve the individual's earlier and later selves (i.e., her diachronic selves) and have consequences for her later self. Compared to our synchronic relationships with other people or our synchronic relationship with ourselves, diachronic self-regarding decisions have two distinctive traits. First, when we make a diachronic self-regarding decision, we do not know whether our future selves will agree and be happy with that choice. Second, one party in a diachronic self-regarding decision—namely, our future selves—cannot take part into the decision, even though the decision primarily affects our future selves.

This book stems from the need to better understand our relationships with our future selves in diachronic self-regarding decisions and offers insights regarding how to make the right choice for ourselves in such decisions. The book addresses the biological reasons why we tend to overlook our future selves; analyzes the moral features of the relationship between our present and future selves; and identifies the responsibilities, rights, and duties that a person's earlier and later selves have to one another. To guide individuals in making the right choices for their future selves, I deal with diachronic self-regarding decisions from the perspective of one's present self, who is

DOI: 10.4324/9781003122142-1

the subject making the decision. The temporal distance between a person's present and future selves depends on the diachronic self-regarding decision at stake.

Self-regarding decisions are a matter of *prudence*. I broadly conceive of prudence as care of oneself that aspires to the good life, also called "well-being" in philosophy. Whereas the philosophical literature on prudence has mainly focused on well-being, in this book, I deal with care for oneself understood as the protection of one's future agency (i.e., the capacity to be an agent). The scope of this book is not the good life in its entirety, but rather the care for oneself in diachronic self-regarding decisions and the moral requirements descending therefrom. Compared to the care for others, the care for oneself has been relatively neglected in moral philosophy,[1] but it is highly relevant to everyone's lives, as the decisions that we make in the present and that have consequences in the future influence our future selves' good life. In such situations, there is often the risk—and doubt, from our first-person perspective—that what we take care of and consider the right thing to do at present may oppose that which we may take care of and consider the right thing to do in the future.

When we talk about morality, we usually refer to *other-regarding morality* (Neblett 1969, 71; Timmermann 2006, 505; Schmidtz 1997, 107), which concerns other individuals' good, not our own. In contrast, *self-regarding morality* regulates the individual's relationship with herself. Diachronic self-regarding decisions are part of self-regarding morality. In moral philosophy, one's relationship with oneself has attracted less interest than other-regarding morality because, since Kant, morality has mainly been considered other-regarding and interpersonal (i.e., regulating the relationships among persons) (Annas 1995; Den Uyl 1991, chs. 1, 6). In Kant's view, prudence is a self-interested behavior that consists of seeking one's own happiness (Kant 2006 [1785], 4:416: 27; Den Uyl 1991, ch. 6) and it is not moral, as people naturally seek their own happiness. Liberalism contributed to the overlooking of self-regarding morality. A cornerstone of the liberal tradition is that, since the individual is an autonomous being, her actions with consequences only on herself are always morally permitted (Mill 2003 [1859], chs. 4–5). By contrast, in ancient (e.g., Greek) ethical theories, prudence—meant as the care for one's own good—was considered moral (Annas 1995, 241, 244–45) and was even the first order of concern in ethics (Den Uyl 1991, 5, 20).

The book proposes two theories. The first is the *overarching intertemporal-choice theory of the perceived future self*, which is an empirical theory of prudential perception: it describes how individuals perceive their future selves in *intertemporal choices* (ICs). ICs are a simplified version of diachronic self-regarding decisions that can be more easily empirically investigated, as I explain below. My empirical theory of prudential perception connects and integrates current intertemporal-choice theories concerning the perception of one's future self, based on the behavioral and neuroscientific studies on such a perception. These studies show that individuals tend to perceive their future selves as distinct from themselves and on par with other individuals (Pronin and Ross 2006; Pronin et al. 2008; Nussbaum et al. 2003; Mitchell et al. 2006; Ersner-Hershfield et al. 2009).

As the diachronic self-regarding decisions that we face in our lives cannot be investigated in laboratory environments, I focus on ICs to study the neurobehavioral basis of our perceptions of our future selves. ICs can be viewed as experimentally observable diachronic self-regarding decisions. ICs are characterized by a short-term, smaller option and a long-term, larger one. When we choose between eating delicious, unhealthy food and tasteless, healthy food, we face an IC. The first option provides immediate gratification but has negative health consequences over the long term, while the second option is less pleasurable but offers greater future benefits, such as the reduction of the risk of some noncommunicable diseases. People usually temporally discount the choice options in ICs, namely, they devalue the outcome as a function of its delayed nature.

The second theory elaborated in this book is the *Moral Theory of Prudence in diachronic self-regarding decisions*, which prescribes how individuals should treat their future selves. It is a normative theory that indicates the rights and duties that the present and the future selves have to each other. This theory derives from the moral features of the relationship between one's present and future selves and is constrained by a model of one's selves as practical agents. I conceive of the practical agent as a subject who is able to take actions for which she can provide reasons and is situated at a temporal stage of a person and coexists with the person. This practical agent can be considered a morally relevant attribute of the person but cannot be conceived of as an entity metaphysically distinct from the person. Compared to several theories of prudence, which are grounded on well-being (Cureton 2016; Arvan 2020; McKerlie 2007; Pettigrew 2020), the main novelty of mine consists in being grounded on the agency of the diachronic (i.e., past, present, and future) selves of a person.

Structure of the book

This book is organized into four chapters. In Chapter 1, I answer the question: "How do we perceive our future selves in intertemporal choices?" I discuss how individuals tend to perceive their future selves, on the basis of the neurobehavioral studies on the topic. I present studies showing that individuals tend to perceive their future selves as distinct persons and that they make suboptimal (i.e., bad) ICs when they have such perceptions. I then describe the theories explaining the individuals' perceptions of their future selves. Each of these theories attributes temporal discounting to an aspect of such a perception: psychological continuity with the future self, adoption of her perspective, and mental construal of the future self. I argue that the theories of the perception of the future self are not mutually exclusive and indicate their interrelations. I identify the main principles of the overarching intertemporal-choice theory of the perceived future self.

In Chapter 2, I answer the question: "What is the nature of the relationship in which we stand with our future selves?" In analyzing this relationship, I tackle two topics: one's care of oneself (i.e., prudence) and the identity relation between an individual's present and future selves. Regarding the first topic, I discuss the main views on the morality of prudence in moral philosophy and contend that prudence is a moral requirement. Regarding the second topic, the relevant entities in the relationship between the present and future selves can be described on two levels. The first is the metaphysical level and regards the person, and the second is practical and concerns the agent. To be effective in the sphere of action, we need not know what we are at the metaphysical level; rather we need only a practical concept of ourselves (Korsgaard 1989, 110–11; Morton 2013, 812). Hence, I focus on the practical level and outline a minimal, realistic model of the agent as a practical, rather than metaphysical, entity, which I describe as a "self." In this model, the subject facing a diachronic self-regarding decision is a practical entity situated at a temporal stage of the person, who is a metaphysical entity. The essential components of this practical agent are: a *set of normative principles of actions* that provide her with reasons for action; her extension over a certain period of time, which does not necessarily coincide with the person's life of which the agent is a part; and care for the person's future self, which depends on the agent's perceived connection with the future self. I analyze the present-self–future-self relationship and identify its moral features. I argue that this relationship has a structure of decisional power, freedom, and knowledge that resembles that of the relationship between contemporary people and future generations. Accordingly, I interpret diachronic self-regarding decisions as a special case of intergenerational ethics.

In Chapter 3, I answer the question: "How should we treat our future selves?" My conception of prudence as moral, the minimal, realistic model of the agent, and the moral features of the present-self–future-self relationship identified in Chapter 2 provide the theoretical basis for this chapter's elaboration of the Moral Theory of Prudence. This theory regulates the relationship between the individual's earlier and later selves in diachronic self-regarding decisions. It mainly states that we have a moral obligation in the present to respect our future selves' rights to be an agent, which means the future selves' freedom to pursue their sets of normative principles. Such an obligation requires us to avoid choices that jeopardize the necessary conditions (e.g., health, adequate educations, basic rights) for the pursuit of any set of normative principles in the future. I defend the Moral Theory of Prudence against objections stemming from its focus on one's diachronic selves (e.g., the impossibility of ascribing moral claims to the future self, who does not yet exist) and against objections specific to the moral requirements of my theory (e.g., the alleged impossibility of having duties to oneself). I discuss the alternative approaches to diachronic self-regarding decisions and explain the difference between those positions and my own. I also contend that in my approach to diachronic self-regarding decisions, prudence is a moral requirement because it demands the protection of a fundamental basis of morality, namely agency, in the relationship between one's earlier and later selves.

In Chapter 4, I answer the question: "How does the Moral Theory of Prudence work in practice?" First, I apply the theory to Parfit's thought experiment of the nineteenth-century Russian nobleman, which is a diachronic self-regarding decision. I then apply the theory to advance healthcare directives in the case of dementia. A patient affected by this disease usually does not drastically lose decision-making capacity and could still retain agency while she is declared incompetent. I refute the *personal identity problem*—the thesis that, in dementia, advance directives are not morally valid because the author of the advance directives is metaphysically different from the patient subject to them due to psychological shifts (Dresser 1986, 1995). I adopt a different approach from which to view the identity relationship between the person writing the advance directives and the person subject to them: the model of the practical agent. In this model, the changes in the person affected with dementia are qualitative, as they are changes within the same person and do not give rise to a numerically different person. The Moral Theory of Prudence applies to advance directives as long as the patient who is subject to an advance directive is an agent or is presumed to be such. This theory requires shifting the criterion for assessing the validity of advance directives from personal identity to agency.

Note

1. To delve into the main contributions to the investigation of the care for oneself, see Aristotle (2000, book VI, chapter 5), Smith (1976 [1790], part VI, sect. i) [1790], Parfit (1984, chs. 14, 15), Den Uyl (1991), Annas (1995), Brink (2003), Bruckner (2003), McKerlie (2007), Cureton (2016), Arvan (2020), Pettigrew (2020), and Dorsey (2021).

References

Annas, Julia. 1995. "Prudence and Morality in Ancient and Modern Ethics." *Ethics* 105: 241–57.

Aristotle. 2000. *Nichomachean Ethics*. Edited by R. Crisp. Cambridge: Cambridge University Press. https://doi.org/10.7208/chicago/9780226026763.001.0001.

Arvan, Marcus. 2020. *Neurofunctional Prudence and Morality*. New York: Routledge.

Brink, David O. 2003. "Prudence and Authenticity: Intrapersonal Conflicts of Value." *Philosophical Review* 112 (2): 215–45. https://doi.org/10.1215/00318108-112-2-215.

Bruckner, Donald W. 2003. "A Contractarian Account of (Part of) Prudence." *American Philosophical Quarterly* 40 (1): 33–46. https://doi.org/10.2307/20010095.

Cureton, Adam. 2016. "Prudence and Responsibility to Self in an Identity Crisis." *Res Philosophica* 93 (4): 815–41. https://doi.org/10.11612/resphil.1466.

Den Uyl, Douglas J. 1991. *The Virtue of Prudence*. New York: Peter Lang.

Dorsey, Dale. 2021. *A Theory of Prudence*. Oxford University Press. https://doi.org/10.1093/oso/9780198823759.001.0001.

Dresser, Rebecca. 1986. "Life, Death, and Incompetent Patients: Conceptual Infirmities and Hidden Values in the Law." *Arizona Law Review* 28 (3): 373–405.

———. 1995. "Dworkin on Dementia: Elegant Theory, Questionable Policy." *Hastings Center Report* 25 (6): 32–38. https://doi.org/10.2307/3527839.

Ersner-Hershfield, Hal, M. Tess Garton, Kacey Ballard, Gregory R. Samanez-Larkin, and Brian Knutson. 2009. "Don't Stop Thinking About Tomorrow: Individual Differences in Future Self-Continuity Account for Saving." *Judgment and Decision Making* 4 (4): 280–86.

Kant, Immanuel. 2006 [1785]. *Groundwork of the Metaphysics of Morals*. Edited by M. J. Gregor. Cambridge: Cambridge University Press.

Korsgaard, Christine M. 1989. "Personal Identity and the Unity of Agency: A Kantian Response to Parfit." *Philosophy & Public Affairs* 18 (2): 101–32.

McKerlie, Dennis. 2007. "Rational Choice, Changes in Values Over Time, and Well-Being." *Utilitas* 19 (1): 51–72. https://doi.org/10.1017/S0953820806002342.

Mill, John Stuart. 2003 [1859]. "On Liberty." In *Utilitarianism and On Liberty*, edited by M. Warnock. Malden, MA: Blackwell Publishing.

Mitchell, Jason P., C. Neil Macrae, and Mahzarin R. Banaji. 2006. "Dissociable Medial Prefrontal Contributions to Judgments of Similar and Dissimilar Others." *Neuron* 50 (4): 655–63. https://doi.org/10.1016/J.NEURON.2006.03.040.

Morton, Jennifer M. 2013. "Deliberating for Our Far Future Selves." *Ethical Theory and Moral Practice*. https://doi.org/10.1007/s10677-012-9391-2.

Neblett, William. 1969. "Morality, Prudence, and Obligations to Oneself." *Ethics* 80 (1): 70–73. https://doi.org/10.1086/291752.

Nussbaum, Shiri, Yaacov Trope, and Nira Liberman. 2003. "Creeping Dispositionism: The Temporal Dynamics of Behavior Prediction." *Journal of Personality and Social Psychology* 84 (3): 485–97. https://doi.org/10.1037/0022-3514.84.3.485.

Parfit, Derek. 1984. *Reasons and Persons*. Oxford: Clarendon Press.

Pettigrew, Richard. 2020. *Choosing for Changing Selves*. Oxford: Oxford University Press.
Pronin, Emily, Christopher Y. Olivola, and Kathleen A. Kennedy. 2008. "Doing Unto Future Selves As You Would Do Unto Others: Psychological Distance and Decision Making." *Personality and Social Psychology Bulletin* 34 (2): 224–36. https://doi.org/10.1177/0146167207310023.
Pronin, Emily, and Lee Ross. 2006. "Temporal Differences in Trait Self-Ascription: When the Self Is Seen as an Other." *Journal of Personality and Social Psychology* 90 (2): 197–209. https://doi.org/10.1037/0022-3514.90.2.197.
Schmidtz, David. 1997. "Self-interest: What's in it for Me?" *Social Philosophy and Policy* 14 (1): 107–21. https://doi.org/10.1017/S0265052500001692.
Smith, A. 1976 [1790]. "The Theory of Moral Sentiments." In *The Glasgow Edition of the Works and Correspondence of Adam Smith*, edited by D. D. Raphael and A. L. Macfie, Vol. I. Oxford: Clarendon Press.
Timmermann, Jens. 2006. "Kantian Duties to the Self, Explained and Defended." *Philosophy* 81 (317): 505–30.

1 How do we perceive our future selves? The neurobehavioral basis of one's perception of the future self

1. Introduction

In this chapter, I address how the individuals tend to perceive their future selves, based on the neurobehavioral studies on the topic conducted on a simplified version of diachronic self-regarding decisions, and describe the theories explaining individuals' perceptions of their future selves in such decisions. I then integrate these theories by applying the findings on empathy and perspective taking to the individual's perception of her future self. Finally, I outline the *overarching intertemporal-choice theory of the perceived future self*, which integrates and connects the aspects of one's perception of the future self that are identified by the aforementioned theories.

The diachronic self-regarding decisions that we face in our lives, such as career choices, cannot be studied in laboratory environments and include many factors and determinants that are not easily modeled in experimental settings. Accordingly, in this chapter, I focus on a simplified and experimentally observable kind of diachronic self-regarding decisions: intertemporal choices (ICs). ICs are decisions that have consequences at different points in time and involve a trade-off related to the magnitude of the outcome and the time at which the outcome is received. A clear example of an IC is the choice between delicious, unhealthy food that provides immediate gratification but increases the long-term risk of some diseases (e.g., diabetes, some heart diseases, stroke, and some cancers) and tasteless, healthy food that has long-term health benefits (e.g., prevention of certain noncommunicable diseases and longer life span) but is less gratifying.[1] Another example of an IC is deciding between leisurely recreation and dedication to a task that guarantees better career options over the long term. ICs are characterized by a short-term, smaller (henceforth, "sooner smaller") option and a long-term, larger (henceforth, "later larger") one. The typical behavior observed in response to ICs in both animals and humans is *temporal discounting*: the devaluing of rewards as a function of their delayed nature. For instance, people usually prefer €10 in cash that is immediately available over a €15 check that can be cashed in one year, even though the value of the check is higher and the check is thus the optimal choice. The steeper an individual's discounting, the more she is impatient, thus likely to choose the sooner smaller reward. Over the long term, steep temporal discounting can bring about negative effects such as overeating, diseases deriving from a sedentary lifestyle, and poor education.

As ICs involve one's future self, how the individual perceives her future self is relevant for the theories dealing with ICs. The theories dealing with the descriptive level of ICs, namely how agents *do* make ICs, have identified many factors that determine temporal discounting. These include impulsivity (Mischel 1974; Ainslie 1975; Loewenstein 1996, 2000), the framing of the delivery time (Read et al. 2005; Lewis and Oyserman 2015), the framing of the options (Jenkins and Hsu 2017; Loewenstein et al. 1998; Liberman and Trope 2003; Trope and Liberman 2003), the mental simulation of the future outcome (Peters and Büchel 2010; Daniel et al. 2013a, 2013b; Benoit et al. 2011; Dassen et al. 2016), the prediction of future emotions and preferences (Gilbert and Wilson 2007; Loewenstein et al. 2003; Wilson and Gilbert 2003, 2005), the subjective perception of the duration between time points (Kim and Zauberman 2019), and asymmetrical attention to the opportunity costs of the sooner versus later rewards (Read et al. 2017).

Several behavioral and neuroscientific studies have shown that how an individual perceives her future self strongly influences her ICs. In particular, when an individual perceives her future self as distinct from her present self,[2] she will have a steeper temporal discounting rate (Bartels and Urminsky 2011, 2015; Ersner-Hershfield et al. 2009a, 2009b; Hershfield et al. 2011; Mitchell et al. 2011; Pronin et al. 2008). On the basis of such evidence, some descriptive theories on ICs regarding the individual's perception of her future self have been proposed, which I call *IC theories of the perceived future self*. These theories are the *future self-continuity model* (Hershfield 2011, 2019; Hershfield and Bartels 2018), the *simulation model of intertemporal preferences* (O'Connell et al. 2015), and the application of the *construal level theory* (Trope and Liberman 2010, 2003; Liberman and Trope 2003) to the perception of the future self and future reward. Before presenting the IC theories of the perceived future self, I introduce the studies concerning how people perceive their future selves and explain why I apply the findings on perspective taking and empathy to the investigation of one's perception of one's future self.

2. Behavioral and neuroscientific studies on the perception of the future self

I will focus on studies of healthy adults, who are the most studied subjects in the domain of the perception of one's future self.[3] In behavioral studies, subjects tended to treat their future selves as they would treat another person. In self-ascription tasks, participants attributed fewer personality traits to their present selves than to their future selves or to another person (Jones and Nisbett 1972; Pronin and Ross 2006). In visual imagery tasks, participants adopted an actor (i.e., first-person) perspective for their present selves and an observer (i.e., third-person) perspective for their future selves and other people (Pronin and Ross 2006). In explaining someone else's behavior, subjects attributed more global, general causes to events happening to them in the distant future or to events happening to other people than to events happening to them in the near future (Nussbaum et al. 2003). The treatment of the future self as another person has also been found in ICs with various outcomes. For instance, subjects discounted the present self's money more steeply than money belonging to their future selves or to another person, chose larger quantities of a distasteful liquid to be drunk by their future selves or by another person than by their present selves, and assigned more hours of voluntary work to their future selves or another person than to their present selves (Pronin et al. 2008). However, Molouki and Bartels (2020) found that, in resources allocation tasks, the amount of money that subjects assigned to their future selves was greater than what they assigned to other people. Yet, the decision-making processes determining resource allocation to the future self and to other people were found to be the same.[4] Therefore, this study does not undermine the aforementioned findings. It is possible that, although the individual perceives her future self as distinct from herself, she still feels that the latter is closer to her than are other people. Moreover, while the investigation of how the individual treats the future self in resource-allocation tasks is important for the investigation of how the individual's present self perceives the future self, it reveals only one aspect of the relationship between the present and future selves. Empirical insights into such a relationship also come from studies on self-ascription, visual imagery, and behavior explanation, which all reveal, as just seen, that subjects treat their future selves and other people in a similar way, but differently from how they treat their present selves.

A neuroscientific study has shown that individuals tend to perceive their future selves as another person at the neural level. Mitchell et al. (2011) had subjects perform both an IC task and an affective forecasting task, in which subjects predicted how much they or another person would have enjoyed engaging in a series of activities either in the present or a year later. When thinking about their future selves (self-future trials), subjects showed less activity in the ventromedial prefrontal cortex (VMPFC)[5] than when they predicted how much they would have enjoyed present events (self-present trials). The greater the activation difference in the VMPFC between the present and future trials, the less patient the subjects were in the IC task. Moreover, activity in the VMPFC was similar when subjects predicted the enjoyment of their future self and that of other people. This level of activity was lower than the level in the self-present trials (i.e., when subjects assessed their own enjoyment of a present activity).[6]

3. Application of the findings on perspective taking and empathy to the study of the perception of the future self

Since the studies described so far indicate that the future self and other people are perceived similarly, I contend that studies on perspective taking and empathy, if applied to the future self, could offer some insight into the subjective perceptions of the future self and, in turn, into ICs. Perspective taking consists of imagining being another person, evaluating her mental state, and appraising the situation in which she finds herself (Decety and Lamm 2006; Batson 2009). This capacity is based on *theory of mind* (ToM) or *mentalizing*—that is, the ability to infer and represent another person's mental state (Singer and Tusche 2014). Perspective taking requires the ability to represent the self as distinct from the other person and the awareness that the other person's state does not necessarily correspond to one's own state. It is a fundamental component of top-down empathy (Decety and Lamm 2006), as it gives inputs to nonreflexive and automatic levels of empathy. Empathy is the ability to share the feelings of others and comprises the empathizer's awareness that the target's feelings elicit the empathizer's response. It is an affective state that is isomorphic to the target's affective state and is elicited by observing or imagining the latter (Singer and Tusche 2014).

My application of the findings on perspective taking and empathy to the perception of the future self in ICs is based on studies regarding *episodic future thinking* in ICs and the self-projection system. Episodic future thinking or mental time travel to the future is the ability to project the self forward in time to pre-experience events (Atance and O'Neill 2001; Tulving 1985). This ability requires ToM, as the subject must be able to differentiate between her present mental state and her future self's mental state (Suddendorf and Corballis 1997, 2007). When prompted in ICs, episodic future thinking decreases temporal discounting (Peters and Büchel 2010; Daniel et al. 2013a, 2013b; Benoit et al. 2011; Dassen et al. 2016). Interestingly, episodic future thinking and ToM share a common pattern of neural activation (Spreng and Grady 2010; Spreng et al. 2009). Buckner and Carroll (2007) propose that they are based on the same cognitive process, namely self-projection: the shift of perspective from the immediate present to alternative perspectives. In section 6 of this chapter, I will show that the findings of the studies on perspective taking and empathy enable the interrelation of the three IC theories of the perceived future self, which I will describe and discuss next.

4. IC theories of the perceived future self

Three IC theories deal with the individual's perception of her future self: the future self-continuity model, the simulation model of intertemporal preferences, and the application of the construal level theory to the future self and future reward. Although the latter theory relates to intertemporal changes of values, it can be applied to the perception of the future self, if the individual's motivation is considered a proxy of the value of (i.e., the worth attributed to) an outcome, as I will show in section 4.3.

4.1 Future self-continuity model

The future self-continuity model explains temporal discounting by means of the individual's *psychological continuity* with the future self. Parfit introduced the concept of psychological continuity to indicate the overlapping of psychological states (e.g., memories, preferences, plans) between two or more individuals in the debate over personal identity. If one perceives a very weak connection with one's future self, then one perceives one's future self as a numerically different person (Parfit 1971, 1984, 318).[7]

In the future self-continuity model, psychological continuity motivates the individual to care about her future self and is a predictor of temporal discounting. The more the individual perceives her future self as psychologically connected to herself, the less she discounts future utilities (Bartels and Urminsky 2011; Hershfield 2011; Hershfield and Bartels 2018; Hershfield 2019). According to the future self-continuity model, the factors that increase future self-continuity, and consequently decrease temporal discounting, are: the perceived similarity with the future self, the vividness with which the future self is pictured, and a positive attitude toward the future self (Hershfield 2011).

Psychological continuity with the future self has mainly been measured as the perceived similarity between one's present and future selves (Ersner-Hershfield et al. 2009a; Bartels and Urminsky 2011, 2015). Perceived similarity is highly correlated with temporal discounting: subjects who perceive their future selves to be similar to their present selves exhibit lower temporal discounting than subjects who perceive their future selves to be dissimilar from their present selves (Ersner-Hershfield et al. 2009a). Furthermore, experimentally increasing psychological continuity (e.g., by priming subjects with a message highlighting the stability of identity over time) has been shown to reduce temporal discounting (Bartels and Urminsky 2011).

The future self-continuity model attributes temporal discounting to perceived low psychological continuity with the future self, not to the perception that the future self is similar to another person. This perception is read as the consequence of low psychological continuity. Within this model, the neurobehavioral results presented in the previous section are interpreted as cases in which the subjects had low psychological continuity with their future selves.

The future self-continuity model does not deal with the mechanisms modulating future self-continuity. However, in some experimental paradigms that Hershfield and colleagues adopted to stimulate subjects' future self-continuity, it is likely that mechanisms of empathy and perspective taking are involved. In a study by Hershfield et al. (2011), subjects seeing their own future selves through age-morphed pictures of their present selves discounted future outcomes less and saved more money for retirement compared with controls. One of the two explanations that the authors provide for this result is that exposure to the future self may have rendered the individual more aware of the future self's emotions and better able to forecast them. The authors connect this hypothesis to the *hot/cold empathy gap theory* (Loewenstein 1996; Loewenstein et al. 1998, 2003). In this theory, when people experience a strong visceral factor, they are described as being in a "hot state;" when they do not experience a strong visceral factor, they are described as being in a "cold state." The empathy gap refers to the tendency of individuals in one state to misrepresent how they would behave in the other. It is possible that the age-progressed renderings of the subjects led them to identify with their future selves, thus reducing the empathy gap. The alternative explanation provided by Hershfield et al. (2011) is that the intervention of the study was more engaging than traditional interventions, and that self-control is enhanced when tasks are engaging (Laran and Janiszewski 2011). However, it is unlikely that Hershfield et al.'s (2011) results are due to how engaging the task was, since similar results have been found in studies using experimental designs with tasks enhancing future self-continuity that were less engaging (e.g., reading a text stating that personal identity remains stable through life (Bartels and Urminsky 2011)).

Hershfield et al. (2012) consider that lack of care for the future self could be due to the difficulty in empathizing with the future self. In that study, the lack of care for the future self was identified with burdening the future self with the negative consequences of one's unethical behavior. Another possibility that the authors indicate is that care for the future self in subjects with high future self-continuity may be due to *self-concept maintenance*: the desire to maintain a positive perception of oneself, which is a determinant of moral actions (Mazar et al. 2008). The latter interpretation could be plausible in a task that is intertemporal and involves the moral consequences of one's own actions, such as the tasks employed by Hershfield et al. (2012). Yet this interpretation is less sound if applied to the usual IC task, which consists of choosing between a sooner smaller reward and a later larger one. While it cannot be excluded that there may exist a further hypothesis explaining the link between future self-continuity and temporal discounting, the hypothesis regarding the identification with the future self in ICs currently seems more plausible than that regarding self-concept maintenance. The mechanisms enabling the identification with other people are the basis of the next theory on the perception of the future self: the simulation model of intertemporal preferences.

4.2 Simulation model of intertemporal preferences

The simulation model of intertemporal preferences interprets ICs as decisions in which an individual makes choices on behalf of her future self by imagining how she would feel if she were the future self (O'Connell et al. 2015). This latter process consists of *mental simulation* (henceforth, simulation) of the future self. Simulation is the imitation, copy, or reproduction of a mental state, event, or process. It is grounded in imagination: a constructive and recursive process that combines episodic and semantic memories and various pieces of information to create a mental representation (Shanton and Goldman 2010; Suddendorf and Corballis 2007). Simulating the future self involves mental time travel to the future and is one of the two forms of perspective taking, as I will show in section 6.1.

The simulation model is the result of combining of the hot/cold empathy gap theory with the idea that the subject's simulation of others is similar to her simulation of the future self. In this model, two mechanisms constitute simulation and are applied to the future self: *simulation efficacy* and *simulation accuracy*. Simulation efficacy is the ability to simulate other people's perspectives and is described by O'Connell et al. (2015) as similar to emotional contagion.[8] Simulation accuracy is the ability to suppress one's own *egocentricity bias*[9] in order to make correct inferences about other people's mental states. Simulation efficacy increases with socially close others (Cheng et al. 2010), whereas simulation accuracy decreases with socially close others (i.e., the egocentricity bias is more difficult to reduce with socially close others than with distant others) (Savitsky et al. 2011; Tamir and Mitchell 2013). O'Connell et al. (2015) parallel social distance from other people with temporal distance from the future self. Thus, they argue that simulation efficacy for the future self decreases with temporal distance, whereas simulation accuracy for the future shows the opposite trend.[10] According to the simulation model, in ICs, when one simulates the future self, one adopts the future self's perspective and simulates the value of the delayed reward that the future self will experience.

The simulation model of intertemporal preferences makes two predictions: (i) an increased delay in receiving a reward will increase a person's simulation accuracy for her future self and (ii) an increased delay in receiving a reward will decrease her simulation efficacy for her future self. In this model, temporal discounting is the result of the degrees of simulation accuracy and efficacy for the future self. As admitted by O'Connell et al. (2015), if the simulation accuracy is more effective with socially and temporally distant individuals, then the simulation model produces a counterintuitive prediction: individuals should exhibit a decreasing temporal discounting as a function of time, since the egocentricity bias should diminish (and simulation accuracy should increase) as a function of time. To avoid creating inconsistency with the empirical evidence, the simulation model assumes that the rate at which the value of future outcomes is reduced by simulation efficacy is greater than the rate at which it is increased by simulation accuracy, thus resulting in temporal discounting. Therefore, the simulation model explains temporal discounting as the result of two opposing mechanisms of simulation.

The simulation model is grounded in studies on ToM and empathy in which the target is another person, not the future self. Regarding simulation efficacy, first, empathy is usually easier to trigger when the target is socially proximal to the subject (Hein et al. 2010) and, second, the neural activations of empathy are different for close versus distant others (Xu et al. 2009; Avenanti et al. 2010; Hein et al. 2010; Meyer et al. 2013). Regarding simulation accuracy, at the behavioral level, subjects had more difficulty disentangling from their own perspective in a communication task when they were paired with a friend than when they were paired with a stranger (Savitsky et al. 2011). Furthermore, subjects used the cognitive process of *anchoring-and-adjustment*[11]—which involves the egocentricity bias—only when the other was perceived as similar; perception of similarity is a proxy of social closeness (Tamir and Mitchell 2013).

The role of simulation accuracy in ICs has been confirmed in neuroscientific studies on the right temporo-parietal junction (TPJ).[12] Through a false-belief task,[13] O'Connell et al. (2018) identified the subject-specific right TPJ cluster involved in overcoming the egocentricity bias and then gave subjects an IC task with hypothetical rewards outside the scanner. O'Connell et al. (2018) found a correlation between temporal discounting in the IC task and activity in the subjects' right TPJ clusters: subjects showing higher right TPJ response in the false-belief task exhibited less steep temporal discounting. In addition, the activation of that area was higher when a subset of subjects chose the delayed reward over the immediate reward in an IC task in the scanner.

Soutschek et al. (2016) showed that a shift of perspective influences temporal discounting by applying inhibitory transcranial magnetic stimulation (TMS) to the right posterior TPJ of subjects engaged in an IC task and an interpersonal decision task. Inhibitory TMS temporally disrupts the functioning of the brain area to which it is applied. In the interpersonal decision task, subjects were asked to choose between a reward option solely for themselves and a reward to be split between themselves and another person, whose social distance varied in the trials. Subjects stimulated with TMS discounted future outcomes more than control subjects. Furthermore, in the interpersonal decision task, the TMS subjects showed higher social discounting (i.e., they more steeply discounted the rewards to be split, meaning that they made more selfish choices) than the control subjects. Soutschek et al. (2016) examined the effect of the temporary disruption of the posterior TPJ in a visual perspective-taking task and found that TMS impaired the subjects' ability to overcome their egocentricity bias. Moreover, the degree of egocentricity bias computed in the perspective-taking task predicted temporal and social discount rates in the IC task and in the interpersonal task, respectively. In Soutschek et al.'s (2020) study, subjects with temporally impaired right TPJ showed steeper temporal discounting than did controls and were slower than the latter in adopting the perspective of their eight-year-older selves and in judging future events compared with past events. In light of this study, it is likely that, in O'Connell et al.'s (2018) study, the right TPJ was more active when subjects delayed a reward because it was involved in the shift of perspective from the individual's present self to her future self, or at least in the shift of the subjects' mental focus to future events.

The simulation model applies the concept of social distance to the future self. According to this model, in the studies in which the subjects treated their future selves as other people, subjects did not empathize with their future selves by simulating the latter's experience. The simulation model attributes the tendency of subjects to treat their future selves as other people to a lack of empathy for their future selves when they simulate the latter's experience.

In the simulation model, suppression of the egocentricity bias determines simulation accuracy. However, social cognition relies on several strategies for mental state inference, which vary based on the features of the social

How do we perceive our future selves? 17

environment. People use the egocentricity bias only with similar others. If the target of simulation is a socially distant person, a different mechanism is involved, namely *stereotyping*, which consists of making social inferences by using implicit beliefs about what a group is like (Ames 2004a, 2004b; Jenkins et al. 2008; Ames et al. 2012).

O'Connell et al. (2015) consider simulation efficacy conceptually similar to emotional contagion. However, their definition of simulation efficacy more closely resembles empathy than emotional contagion, as emotional contagion is an automatic mechanism of mimicry that involves a direct perception of the other person without the awareness that the source of the subject's emotional state is another person (Hatfield et al. 1992). By contrast, in the simulation model, simulation efficacy is conceived of as a process in which, first, the individual does not necessarily perceive the other person directly and, second, she is consciously engaged in a shift of perspective. The simulation model assumes that social and temporal distance are similar in that they are based on the same mechanisms (i.e., empathy and perspective taking). The next IC model of the perception of the future self theorizes why this is the case.

4.3 Construal level theory

Construal level theory concerns the mutual influence between psychological distance and the level of mental construal of objects and events. Psychological distance is the subjective distance of an object from the self in the here and now, which is the reference point. The further away the object is from that reference point, the more it is removed from direct experience and imagined in an abstract way (called *high-level construal*). By contrast, reduced distance of the object from the reference point increases the concreteness of its mental construal (*low-level construal*). Psychological distance comprises four dimensions: spatial, temporal, social, and hypothetical (Trope and Liberman 2010). In construal level theory, all dimensions of psychological distance are correlated in the sense that a cue of distance in one dimension affects the perceived distance of an item in another dimension. In this model, the value an individual assigns to an item is the result of that item's high- and low-level features, and choices are determined by the individual's mental construal of the object rather than by the object itself. The individual chooses the item with more positive low-level features when she is in a low-level mental framework; she chooses the item with more positive high-level features when she is in a high-level mental framework. This is because the level of construal in use makes the object with the more positive features at the corresponding level more salient to the subject and thus more likely to be chosen.

In construal level theory, temporal discounting is explained as an effect of psychological distance in the dimension of time: temporal distance induces a representation of items with abstract, central, and enduring characteristics, while temporal proximity induces a representation of items with more concrete and incidental features (Liberman and Trope 2003; Trope and Liberman 2003). Therefore, in ICs, construal level theory predicts that when the subject is in the low-level mode, she will have steep temporal discounting and thus prefers the sooner smaller reward, as the low-level features of the options (e.g., the details of how they smell or taste) are more prominent for the subject. In contrast, if the subject is in the high-level mode, construal level theory predicts the opposite: she should discount future utilities less steeply and choose the delayed reward. This is because, first, in the reward assessment, temporal distance increases the weight of high-level features (namely, the magnitude of the outcome) and decreases the weight of low-level features (namely, the delay). Second, the induced abstract thinking causes the subject to focus on her global concerns, which facilitates behavioral planning over immediate gratification (Liberman and Trope 2003; Trope and Liberman 2003). Furthermore, as temporal distance and level of mental construal influence each other, and as low-level construal is the individual's default mode (Malkoc et al. 2010; Kim et al. 2013; Yi et al. 2017), construal level theory predicts that a more concrete representation of a future outcome renders it closer in the individual's eyes, thus resulting in more patient choices.

Subjects who were primed to use high-level construal by being asked *why* they would carry out certain actions or by being required to make a choice for a stranger preferred later larger rewards over sooner smaller ones in tasks with various hypothetical rewards (Fujita et al. 2006; Fujita and Han 2009; Fujita 2011; Malkoc et al. 2010; Kim et al. 2013; Yi et al. 2017). Similarly, before the elaboration of construal level theory, Mischel's studies on self-control showed that a successful strategy for lowering subjects' temporal discounting was to have subject focus on abstract characteristics of the item (Mischel 1974; Mischel et al. 1989). Even prompting a concrete construction of the future by asking subjects *how* they would carry out a future focal action results in less discounting in an ICs task (Yi et al. 2017).[14]

Temporal distance was shown to influence the subjective value of the choice options by increasing the saliency of their high-level aspects. In a task of item valuation, subjects were more satisfied with the item with a positive high-level characteristic and a negative low-level characteristic when the purchase was in one year and was thus framed with high-level construal (a radio with good sound quality versus a poorly functioning clock). In contrast, they were more satisfied with the item with a positive low-level characteristic and a negative high-level characteristic when the purchase was in one day and was thus framed with low-level construal (a radio with poor sound quality versus a well-functioning clock) (Trope and Liberman 2000).

Construal level theory predicts intertemporal changes in value, not in the motivation of the subject to discount future outcomes. In experimental psychology and behavioral economics, value is a proxy of the motivation to pursue a goal (Lieberman and Trope 2003).[15] Therefore, construal level theory could be applied in the context of ICs to explain an individual's low motivation for getting the later larger reward and thus for caring about her future self. The low-level characteristics of the sooner smaller reward make such a reward more attractive for the subject, who is in the default low-level mode, and thus motivate her to get the sooner smaller reward.

In construal level theory, the finding that the future self is treated similarly to another person is explained by the correspondence between psychological distance and high-level construal. The observation that subjects assigned fewer fixed traits to their present selves than to their future selves or other people (Jones and Nisbett 1972; Pronin and Ross 2006) is consistent with the prediction in construal level theory that the future self and other people are represented in more abstract terms. A fixed character trait is a central and stable personal attribute and thus belongs to high-level construal. Similarly, the finding that subjects attributed more global and general causes to the behavior of other people and the distant future self than to that of the close future self (Nussbaum et al. 2003) indicates that other people and the future self are described in more abstract terms.

The concept of psychological distance resembles that of psychological continuity in future self-continuity theory in that both indicate the subjective perception of distance from a target. However, there are two differences. First, psychological continuity measures distance in terms of degrees of identity, while psychological distance is a broader concept of distance from the self that does not directly imply identity. Second, in future self-continuity theory, temporal distance usually weakens perceived continuity with the future self, but perceived continuity does not influence perceived temporal distance from the future self. Instead, in construal level theory, social distance and temporal distance influence each other, since all dimensions of psychological distance are related to each other under this framework. Similarity is a major determinant of social distance in the sense that the more similar to herself the subject perceives a person to be, the more she is likely to perceive this person as socially close (see, e.g., Heider 1958; Miller et al. 1998). Thus, as a person's psychological continuity with the future self is mainly measured as her perceived similarity with the latter, psychological continuity could be considered a form of social distance within construal level theory. This observation makes an initial connection between the future self-continuity theory and construal level theory. In the

5. Systematization of the IC theories of the perceived future self

The future self-continuity model holds that temporal discounting is determined by perceived continuity with the future self. The simulation model attributes temporal discounting to a failure to adopt the future self's perspective. Construal level theory indicates that the determinant of temporal discounting is the mental construal of the future self and future reward. Are these theories and their determinants of temporal discounting interrelated? I answer this question in light of the studies on perspective taking and empathy.[16]

In simulation, subjects imagine themselves in someone else's place. They use information related to themselves as the starting point for imagining the other person's state; this strategy makes self-relevant information more accessible and thus more likely to be associated with the target (Davis et al. 1996). As a consequence, simulation increases the subject's perceived similarity with other people. Perceived similarity with the future self increases future self-continuity (Ersner-Hershfield et al. 2009a; Bartels and Urminsky 2011, 2015). By applying the connection between simulation and similarity to the perception of the future self, I contend that adopting the future self's perspective increases the perceived continuity with the future self.[17] At the same time, in the case of mentalizing tasks, it has been shown that perceived similarity with a person induces the adoption of her perspective (i.e., simulation of her mental state) rather than inducing stereotyping (Ames 2004a, 2004b; Galinsky and Moskowitz 2000). This means that when imagining or predicting the mental state of one's own future self, a subject who has high psychological continuity with her future self is more likely to mentally simulate her future self's state, rather than using stereotypes. Accordingly, I argue that future self-continuity makes simulation more likely to occur through perceived similarity. In conclusion, the application of the results of the studies on perspective taking and empathy to the perception of the future self supports the identification of a bidirectional relationship between future self-continuity and simulation (see Fig. 1.1).

As construal level is used to mentally represent an object, it is an aspect of the mental representation of an object. Consequently, as the simulation of the future self is a mental representation of the future self, construal level is a component of simulation (Fig. 1.1)—namely, the degree of abstractness with which the future self is represented. Similarly, construal level is an aspect of the mental representation of the future reward, which can be

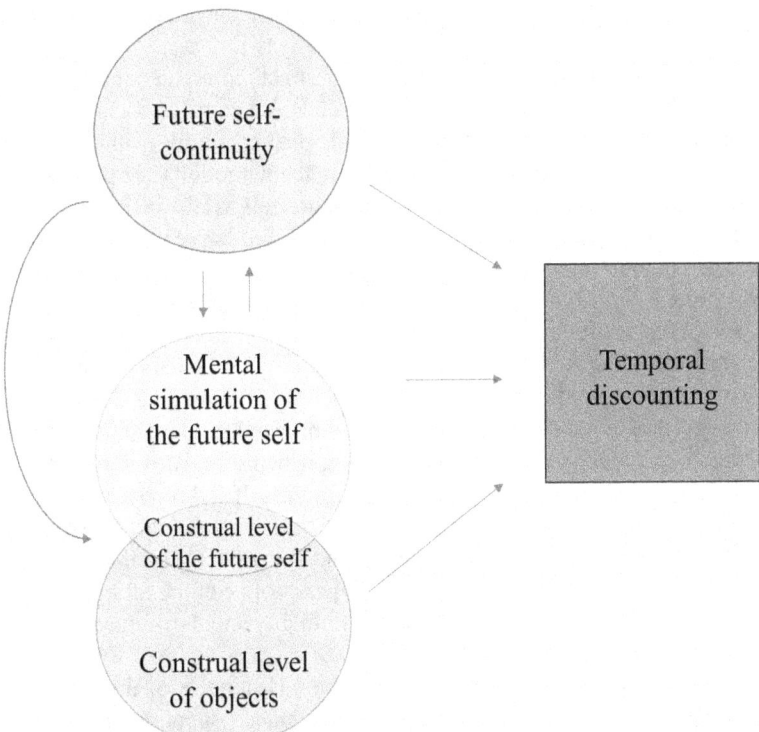

Figure 1.1 Summary scheme of the mutual influences of the determinants of temporal discounting in the IC models of the perceived future self. There is a bidirectional relationship between mental simulation of the future self and future self-continuity. Future self-continuity also affects the construal level of objects, and the latter indirectly affects the former through simulation. Finally, construal level of objects is an aspect of simulation.

framed in either low-level or high-level construal. In studies on inferring other people's mental states, an abstract mindset has been found to increase the use of stereotypes (McCrea et al. 2012), and stereotyping has been found to reduce the adoption of the perspective of the other (Ames 2004b). I thus argue that high-level construal hinders simulation of the future self via the use of stereotypes. On the other hand, simulation could stimulate a low-level mindset as it makes it possible to achieve a more detailed and concrete representation of the target person than the representation that could be arrived at through stereotyping. It is thus plausible that simulation determines a low-level mindset, but no studies have proved this direct influence to date.

As seen, (i) social distance induces an abstract representation of objects, (ii) psychological continuity can be considered a form of social distance from the future self, and (iii) low psychological continuity with the future self corresponds to high social distance from the future self (i.e., one that has low future self-continuity perceives her future self as distinct from herself and thus socially distant). From (i), (ii), and (iii), I derive that low psychological continuity induces an abstract representation of the future self, and psychological continuity thus influences the construal level of the future self (Fig. 1.1). This means that psychological continuity can influence simulation not only directly (as high psychological continuity stimulates simulation) but also indirectly by affecting the construal level of the imagined future self. Low psychological continuity reduces the probability that simulation will be adopted by inducing an abstract mindset, which stimulates stereotyping.

Finally, the level of construal of the future self indirectly affects perceived continuity with the future self through simulation. As seen, an abstract mindset activates stereotyping, and stereotyping inhibits perspective taking. Therefore, the adoption of the perspective of the future self (i.e., simulation)—which increases perceived similarity and thus future self-continuity—is less likely to occur.

In conclusion, I have shown that the three IC models of the perceived future self are not mutually exclusive and indeed support one another: the construal level of the future self or reward is an aspect of simulation. Future self-continuity is a perception that can result from simulation (as the outcome of simulation), and it affects the likelihood that simulation of the future self occurs as well as the construal level of such a simulation.

6. A theory of prudential perception: The overarching IC theory of the perceived future self

On the basis of the review and comparison of the three IC theories of the perceived future self that I have conducted so far, I outline the pillars of the *overarching IC theory of the perceived future self*. This is a descriptive theory that brings together and connects the aspects of an individual's perception of her future self in ICs. As I conceive of prudence as one's care for oneself—which includes one's future self—the overarching IC theory of the perceived future self is an *empirical theory of prudential perception*, namely, it is a theory describing one's perception of one's future self.

Three principles form the pillars of the overarching IC theory of the perceived future self. First, the individual's simulation of her future selves increases her perceived continuity with her future self. Second, the individual's low psychological continuity with her future self decreases the likelihood that she mentally simulates her future self. Third, the individual mentally represents the future self at various degrees of abstractedness (the construal levels), which are influenced by her perceived continuity with her future self.

On the basis of the studies on empathy and perspective taking, in the following sections, I propose three further principles of the overarching IC theory of the perceived future self. These principles can be empirically tested and, if verified, will form part of the overarching IC theory of the perceived future self. The three empirically testable principles are as follows. First, perspective taking reduces temporal discounting only in the form of an *imagine-self perspective* or *imagine-other perspective* in conjunction with high future self-continuity. Second, self-control failure in ICs is due to *weakness of will and imagination*. Third, perspective taking influences ICs because it is also a form of emotion regulation.

6.1 Imagine-self and imagine-other perspectives applied to the future self

The simulation model considers simulation as the only mechanism by which the agent imagines herself in the target's place. However, there are two distinct kinds of perspective taking: the imagine-self perspective and the imagine-other perspective. In the imagine-self perspective, the agent imagines how she would feel if she were in the other person's position. This is the mechanism of simulation considered by O'Connell et al. (2015). In the imagine-other perspective, the agent imagines how she would feel if she were the other, with the other's needs, thoughts, and feelings (Stotland 1969; Batson 2009). Taking this distinction into account can lead to new insights into the IC theories of the perceived future self and, in turn, temporal discounting, as the two kinds of perspective taking bring about different emotional reactions in the subject. In cases wherein the target person is suffering, the imagine-other perspective usually leads to empathic concern: feeling for the other (i.e., an emotional response congruent with the other's plight and devoid of personal distress) and the disposition to help. Conversely, the imagine-self perspective gives rise to personal distress: discomfort as a consequence of seeing the other's plight and withdrawal from aversive arousal (Batson et al. 1987, 1997; Jackson et al. 2006; Lamm et al. 2007).

In ICs, the imagine-other perspective consists of imagining one's future self in the future—who could be perceived as similar or different from one's present self—while the imagine-self perspective consists of imagining one's present self in the future. As the two kinds of perspective taking produce opposite reactions when the target is another person, it is likely that they influence a person's choice in opposite ways even in ICs, where the target is the future self. This reasoning leads to two predictions. When the individual imagines her present self receiving the later larger reward at a future time (imagine-self perspective) and compares her imagined mental state with her present reaction to receiving the sooner smaller reward, she should exhibit low temporal discounting rate. This is because the cost of waiting is null in the simulation of her present self in the future. Therefore, the comparison between the sooner smaller reward and the later larger one involves only the magnitude of the outcome. Consequently, the later larger reward is preferable. In contrast, when the individual imagines her future self at a future time (imagine-other perspective), two reactions may occur depending on her perceived similarity with her future self. If the individual perceives her future self as similar to herself, then the imagine-other perspective is in reality an imagine-self perspective, and thus she should prefer the later larger reward. If the individual perceives her future self as different from herself, she will compare her present reactions to receiving an outcome with the reaction of another individual (i.e., her future self) to a greater outcome in the present. Even here, the simulation nullifies the delay in the comparison, as what is compared are two reactions in the present from the perspective of the individuals receiving the outcome. Yet, in contrast to the case of the imagine-self perspective, here the individuals are not numerically identical: the present self is more salient than the future self from the present self's perspective. The latter hence discounts the future self's utility more steeply and proceeds to choose the sooner smaller reward.

The predictions regarding the effects of the two kinds of perspective taking in ICs could be tested by first measuring the subjects' perceived similarity with their future selves with the psychometric measure of future self-continuity devised by Ersner-Hershfield et al. (2009a), where the present and future selves are each represented as an Euler circle at various degrees of overlappingness with the other one. The subjects would then be assigned ICs with episodic tags of real subject-specific future events,[18] as in Peters and Büchel (2010). The episodic tag usually induces episodic future thinking, which renders the choice of the later larger reward more likely, especially if the subjects have high imagery scores—namely, at the occurrence of the episodic tags, they vividly mentally simulate their future selves (Peters and Büchel 2010). The subjects should perform the IC task in two conditions: imagining their present selves being in their future selves' shoes (imagine-self perspective) and imagining being the future selves (imagine-other perspective).[19] The two conditions should be separated by a few weeks in order to prevent that the first kind of perspective taking adopted influences the condition in which the other kind of perspective taking is adopted. According to my reading, in such a study, subjects with low future self-continuity should be more patient in the imagine-self condition than in the imagine-other condition.

6.2 Self-control failure as weakness of will and imagination

In psychology and economics, overly steep temporal discounting has traditionally been interpreted as a problem of self-control: the individual struggles with the temptation to enjoy immediate gratification (e.g., Mischel 1974; Ainslie 1975; Elster 1979; Thaler and Shefrin 1981; Schelling 1984; Loewenstein 1996). In economics, self-control has been framed as control of multiple selves, each desiring different things (Elster 1979; Thaler and Shefrin 1981; Schelling 1984), or of visceral factors (Loewenstein 1996, 2000). In philosophy, self-control failure is traditionally attributed to weakness of will—that is, acting in a way contrary to one's own present better judgment (e.g., Aristotle 2000, VII, 1–10; Davidson 1980 [1970]; Mele 1987; Holton 1999). In the case of ICs, this means assessing the later larger reward as the best one but choosing the sooner smaller reward. Neuroscientific studies have shown that subjects exert self-control when the brain area that maintains the subject's goals—the lateral prefrontal cortex—upgrades the value of the later larger reward signaled by the VMPFC (Hare et al. 2009; Hare et al. 2011).

Studies on the suppression of the egocentricity bias (Soutschek et al. 2016, 2020; O'Connell et al. 2018) suggest that another form of self-control is also involved in ICs: the change of perspective with the future self that is signaled by the TPJ. As perspective shifts are based on imagination, I read self-control failures in ICs as weakness of imagination. Empirical evidence supports my interpretation. In an IC task with episodic tags, the most patient subjects were those with the highest imagery scores as obtained by measuring the vividness and frequency of episodic future thinking (Peters and Büchel 2010). As Palombo et al. (2015) suggest, there could be two non-mutually exclusive ways in which imagination influences temporal discounting. First, imagination makes the future reward more concrete, which, in turn, may prompt the individual to assign more subjective value to the future reward. Second, imagination makes the rewards closer in subjective time.

My reading of steep temporal discounting in ICs as weakness of imagination is consistent with IC theories of the perceived future self. In future self-continuity theory, in fact, one factor that increases psychological continuity and reduces temporal discounting is the vividness with which the future self is depicted. In the simulation model, the imagination of how one would feel in her future self's place reduces temporal discounting. In construal level theory, construal levels are the frameworks in which the imagined objects are represented.

In future research, the interpretation of steep temporal discounting as failure of imagination could be tested with a between-subjects study comparing the performances of subjects with low versus high imagery scores in two tasks: standard ICs and ICs with episodic tags. In the latter task, the study should also test the correlation between subjects' imagery scores and the occurrence of perspective taking, since, in my hypothesis, imagination is involved in ICs as a shift of perspective from the present self to the future self. According to my reading of steep temporal discounting as weakness of imagination, the high-imagery subjects of the study should make more patient decisions than the low-imagery subjects in the task with episodic tags.

6.3 Perspective taking as a form of emotion regulation

It is likely that perspective taking also contributes to self-control in the form of control of emotions and impulses. Emotion regulation is the ability to override or change one's own inner responses or inhibit undesired impulses. It is one of the strategies that are used to exercise self-control. Distancing is a form of emotion regulation that consists of reinterpreting the meaning of a stimulus by viewing an event from a detached third-person perspective, usually in order to down-regulate an emotion, or from a vivid first-person perspective, usually in order to up-regulate an emotion (Ochsner et al. 2012). Perspective taking is a form of distancing, as the individual can see her present self from a detached position when she adopts the target's perspective. Accordingly, an individual with too steep temporal discounting may fail in distancing—specifically, in seeing herself from a third-person perspective (Viganò 2017). Therefore, I contend that, in ICs, the adoption of the future self's perspective not only makes the future self more vivid and concrete (i.e., it brings the future self closer to the present self) but can also regulate the individual's current emotional state because the individual sees her present self from the future self's perspective. This interpretation could be tested as a complement to the between-subject study on weakness of imagination. I propose to assign the ICs with episodic tags to subjects in a hot state (e.g., hungry subjects that have to make ICs with food items). Self-reporting questionnaires, physiological measures such as skin conductance, and the comparison of neural activations between high-imagery and low-imagery subjects would enable one to verify whether the high-imagery subjects are more detached from present temptations than the low-imagery subjects because the high-imagery subjects' adoption of the future self's perspective facilitates their emotion regulations.[20]

7. Conclusion

ICs are decisions involving a trade-off between the magnitude of an outcome and the time at which the outcome is received. Therefore, they concern and affect one's future self. Understanding how individuals perceive their future selves is relevant for the theories dealing with individuals' behavior in ICs. Neurobehavioral studies have shown that individuals discount future utilities more steeply when they perceive their future selves as distinct from their present selves. The three theories explaining temporal discounting in the light of how the individual perceives her future self indicate that temporal discounting is determined by perceived continuity with the future self's identity (future self-continuity theory), the adoption of her perspective (simulation theory), and the mental construal of the future self and future reward (construal level theory). In this chapter, I argued that these three theories are interrelated and support each other. Construal level of the future self is a component of simulation. Future self-continuity is a perception that can result from simulation and, in turn, affects the likelihood that simulation of the future self occurs. In addition, future self-continuity affects the construal level of objects, and the latter indirectly affects the former through simulation. I outlined the overarching IC theory of the perceived future self, which is my empirical theory of prudential perception. This theory gathers together and connects the aspects of an individual's perception of her future self that lead her to care less for her future self than her present self in ICs. The three pillars of the overarching IC theory of the perceived future self are based on my analysis of the interrelations among the IC theories of the perceived future self.

As the perception of the future self is grounded in mechanisms that individuals employ to understand other people's feelings and mental states (empathy and perspective taking), I applied these mechanisms to the adoption of the future self's perspective in ICs and provided three empirically testable principles. If the latter will be confirmed by empirical studies, they will be included in the overarching IC theory of the perceived future self. The first principle holds that perspective taking reduces temporal discounting only if it is in the form of imagine-self perspective or imagine-other perspective with high future self-continuity. The second principle holds that self-control failure in ICs is due to weakness of will and imagination. The third principle holds that, in ICs, perspective taking is a source of self-control in the form of distancing from the present self.

The subject of this chapter—namely, the empirical studies and theories on individuals' perceptions of their future selves—touches upon a long-debated issue in philosophy: personal identity. What does it mean to perceive one's future self as distinct from one's present self? In the next chapter, I answer this question by dealing with the practical identity of one's earlier and later selves.

Notes

1. See, for instance, World Health Organization (2013), Fuhrman (2018).
2. See Chapter 2 for the identity relation between one's present and future selves.
3. As I am interested in the subjects' perceptions of their future selves, I exclude from my analysis studies on *metacognition*, namely, the awareness and monitoring of one's own thinking, which targets one's present self.
4. The decision-making processes underlying the allocation of resources to the future self or to other people both involve the characteristics of need, deservingness, liking, and similarity of the allocation target. These characteristics have a comparable influence on the allocation of resources between the individual and her future self, on the one hand, and the individual and other people, on the other hand.
5. The VMPFC signals the value of choice options (Rangel and Clithero 2014; Delgado et al. 2016) and is part of the network that is activated in the mental simulation of events occurring in one's own personal future and in remembering personal events (Benoit and Schacter 2015; Schacter et al. 2017).
6. Ersner-Hershfield et al. (2009b) found that the rostral anterior cingulate cortex was activated for the present self but not for the future self and its activity correlated with temporal discounting. However, this area is not relevant for ICs because, as observed by Mitchell et al. (2011), the statistical criteria used in its functional localization were lenient.
7. With the exception of Hershfield and Bartels (2018), the studies on future self-continuity have used the expressions *psychological connectedness* and *psychological continuity* interchangeably. Parfit considered psychological continuity as the overlapping of psychological features between nonconsecutive phases of life (e.g., between the 10-year-old self and the 30-year-old self) and psychological connectedness as the overlapping of psychological features between consecutive phases of life (e.g., between the 10-year-old self and the 11-year-old self). In what follows, I use the expression "psychological continuity" to indicate the individual's perception of overlapping psychological features between her present and future selves, which can be assessed between any two life stages. See also Chapter 2, section 2.2.
8. Emotional contagion is the tendency to be influenced by another person's emotional state without awareness of this influence.
9. Egocentricity bias is the erroneous projections of one's own feelings, thoughts, and beliefs onto other people. To make accurate predictions about others' mental states, it is crucial to control this bias.
10. Simulation accuracy is the ability to suppress one's egocentricity bias; in the case of simulation accuracy for one's future self, the egocentricity bias refers to the erroneous projection of the mental state of one's present self onto one's future self.
11. In anchoring-and-adjustment, the subject infers another person's mental state by using her own perspective as a reference point and then correcting away from that starting point on the basis of the characteristics of the target and context.
12. The TPJ is a brain region involved in ToM, false-belief tasks (see note 13) (Igelström and Graziano 2017; Krall et al. 2015; Schurz et al. 2014), and attention reorienting (Chang et al. 2013; Krall et al. 2015). Geng and Vossel (2013) contend that the TPJ has the broader role of updating internal mental models of the environment or other people.

13. The false-belief task consists of making inferences about the beliefs of people who have information different from that held by the subject performing the task.
14. More precisely, in that study, the results were significant when the change of construal level followed the order that the authors termed *default-then-switch*: in the case of the concrete construction of the future (which is unusual), a reduction in temporal discounting was observed in the sessions in which the subjects were asked to firstly imagine the present in concrete ways and then the future in concrete ways. In the case of the abstract construction of the present (which is unusual, as well), a reduction in temporal discounting was observed in the sessions in which the subjects were asked to firstly imagine the future in abstract ways and then the present in abstract ways.
15. It is noteworthy that evaluation and motivation are conceptually different from a theoretical perspective, as one can be more or less motivated to pursue a goal with the value of the goal remaining the same.
16. See section 3 for the reasons I apply these studies to the investigation of one's perception of the future self.
17. McCarroll and Cosentino (2020) offer a different explanation of the effect of simulation on psychological continuity and, in turn, on temporal discounting. Simulating the perspective of a socially or temporally distant target usually induces a person to view the target from a detached, third-person perspective. They argue that, in the case of an individual imagining her future self, the third-person perspective leads the individual to mentally represent the future self in a high-level mode (i.e., in abstract terms such as character traits). Since the authors contend that character traits are a key aspect of psychological continuity, they argue that the adoption of the third-person perspective increases the individual's perceived psychological continuity with her future self and decreases the steepness of her temporal discounting. However, in Peters and Büchel's (2010) study, the reports of the subjects with low temporal discounting imagining their future selves were vivid and detailed, thus suggesting that the simulation of their future selves was in a low-level mode. This conflicts with McCarroll and Cosentino's explanation. In addition, psychological continuity is not necessarily a high-level element. Psychological continuity has been measured not only with character traits attribution (Bartels and Urminsky 2011) but also with a psychometric measure of future self-continuity quantifying the individual's intuitive perception of similarity between her present and future selves, each represented as an Euler circle at various degrees of overlappingness with the other (Ersner-Hershfield et al. 2009a; Hershfield et al. 2012).
18. In ICs with episodic tags, subjects are shown not only the amount of the choice option and the time at which it is delivered but also a verbal label indicating what event they had planned on the day of the reward delivery.
19. The order in which the two conditions are assigned to the subjects should be randomly selected.
20. When distancing from oneself by adopting the perspective of one's future self, it is conceivable that the imagine-other and the imagine-self perspectives activate different degrees of emotion regulation. They both enable one to see oneself from distance, but it is likely that the maximum degree of emotion regulation is reached when the subject adopts the imagine-other perspective and has low future self-continuity. This is because viewing oneself from the perspective of somebody that is perceived as distinct from oneself makes possible a detachment from one's emotions that is higher than that induced by viewing oneself from the perspective of oneself in a different time (i.e., in the future).

References

Ainslie, George. 1975. "Specious Reward: A Behavioral Theory of Impulsiveness and Impulse Control." *Psychological Bulletin* 82 (4): 463–96. https://doi.org/10.1037/h0076860.

Ames, Daniel R. 2004a. "Inside the Mind Reader's Tool Kit: Projection and Stereotyping in Mental State Inference." *Journal of Personality and Social Psychology* 87 (3): 340–53. https://doi.org/10.1037/0022-3514.87.3.340.

———. 2004b. "Strategies for Social Inference: A Similarity Contingency Model of Projection and Stereotyping in Attribute Prevalence Estimates." *Journal of Personality and Social Psychology* 87 (5): 573–85. https://doi.org/10.1037/0022-3514.87.5.573.

Ames, Daniel R., Elke U. Weber, and Xi Zou. 2012. "Mind-Reading in Strategic Interaction: The Impact of Perceived Similarity on Projection and Stereotyping." *Organizational Behavior and Human Decision Processes* 117 (1): 96–110. https://doi.org/10.1016/J.OBHDP.2011.07.007.

Aristotle. 2000. *Nichomachean Ethics*. Edited by R. Crisp. Cambridge: Cambridge University Press. https://doi.org/10.7208/chicago/9780226026763.001.0001.

Atance, Cristina M., and Daniela K. O'Neill. 2001. "Episodic Future Thinking." *Trends in Cognitive Sciences* 5 (12): 533–39. https://doi.org/10.1016/S1364-6613(00)01804-0.

Avenanti, Alessio, Angela Sirigu, and Salvatore M. Aglioti. 2010. "Racial Bias Reduces Empathic Sensorimotor Resonance with Other-Race Pain." *Current Biology* 20 (11): 1018–22. https://doi.org/10.1016/j.cub.2010.03.071.

Bartels, Daniel M., and Oleg Urminsky. 2011. "On Intertemporal Selfishness: How the Perceived Instability of Identity Underlies Impatient Consumption." *Journal of Consumer Research* 38 (1): 182–98. https://doi.org/10.1086/658339.

———. 2015. "To Know and to Care: How Awareness and Valuation of the Future Jointly Shape Consumer Spending." *Journal of Consumer Research* 41 (6): 1469–85. https://doi.org/10.1086/680670.

Batson, C. Daniel. 2009. "Two Forms of Perspective Taking: Imagining How Another Feels and Imagining How You Would Feel." In *Handbook of Imagination and Mental Simulation*, edited by K. D. Markman, W. M. P. Klein, and J. A. Suhr. New York: Psychology Press.

Batson, C. Daniel, Shannon Early, and Giovanni Salvarani. 1997. "Perspective Taking: Imagining How Another Feels Versus Imaging How You Would Feel." *Personality and Social Psychology Bulletin* 23 (7): 751–58. https://doi.org/10.1177/0146167297237008.

Batson, C. Daniel, Jim Fultz, and Patricia A. Schoenrade. 1987. "Distress and Empathy: Two Qualitatively Distinct Vicarious Emotions With Different Motivational Consequences." *Journal of Personality* 55 (1): 19–39.

Benoit, Roland G., Sam J. Gilbert, and Paul W. Burgess. 2011. "A Neural Mechanism Mediating the Impact of Episodic Prospection on Farsighted Decisions." *The Journal of Neuroscience* 31 (18): 6771–79. https://doi.org/10.1523/JNEUROSCI.6559-10.2011.

Benoit, Roland G., and Daniel L. Schacter. 2015. "Specifying the Core Network Supporting Episodic Simulation and Episodic Memory by Activation Likelihood Estimation." *Neuropsychologia* 75: 450–57. https://doi.org/10.1016/J.NEUROPSYCHOLOGIA.2015.06.034.

Buckner, Randy L., and Daniel C. Carroll. 2007. "Self-Projection and the Brain." *Trends in Cognitive Sciences* 11 (2): 49–57. https://doi.org/10.1016/j.tics.2006.11.004.

Chang, Chi-Fu, Tzu-Yu Hsu, Philip Tseng, Wei-Kuang Liang, Ovid J. L. Tzeng, Daisy L. Hung, and Chi-Hung Juan. 2013. "Right Temporoparietal Junction and Attentional Reorienting." *Human Brain Mapping* 34 (4): 869–77. https://doi.org/10.1002/hbm.21476.

Cheng, Yawei, Chenyi Chen, Ching Po Lin, Kun Hsien Chou, and Jean Decety. 2010. "Love Hurts: An FMRI Study." *NeuroImage* 51 (2): 923–29. https://doi.org/10.1016/j.neuroimage.2010.02.047.

Daniel, Tinuke Oluyomi, Christina M. Stanton, and Leonard H. Epstein. 2013a. "The Future Is Now: Reducing Impulsivity and Energy Intake Using Episodic Future Thinking." *Psychological Science* 24 (11): 2339–42. https://doi.org/10.1177/0956797613488780.

Daniel, Tinuke Oluyomi, Christina M. Stanton, and Leonard H. Epstein. 2013b. "The Future Is Now: Comparing the Effect of Episodic Future Thinking on Impulsivity in Lean and Obese Individuals." *Appetite* 71: 120–25.

Dassen, Fania C. M., Anita Jansen, Chantal Nederkoorn, and Katrijn Houben. 2016. "Focus on the Future: Episodic Future Thinking Reduces Discount Rate and Snacking." *Appetite* 96: 327–32. https://doi.org/10.1016/j.appet.2015.09.032.

Davidson, Donald. 1980 [1970]. "How Is Weakness of the Will Possible?" In *Essays on Actions and Events*, edited by D. Davidson. Oxford: Clarendon Press. https://doi.org/10.1093/0199246270.003.0002.

Davis, Mark H., Laura Conklin, Amy Smith, and Carol Luce. 1996. "Effect of Perspective Taking on the Cognitive Representation of Persons: A Merging of Self and Other." *Journal of Personality and Social Psychology* 70 (4): 713–26. https://doi.org/10.1037/0022-3514.70.4.713.

Decety, Jean, and Claus Lamm. 2006. "Human Empathy through the Lens of Social Neuroscience." *The Scientific World Journal* 6: 1146–63.

Delgado, Mauricio R., Jennifer S. Beer, Lesley K. Fellows, Scott A. Huettel, Michael L. Platt, Gregory J. Quirk, and Daniela Schiller. 2016. "Viewpoints: Dialogues on the Functional Role of the Ventromedial Prefrontal Cortex." *Nature Neuroscience* 19 (12): 1545–52. https://doi.org/10.1038/nn.4438.

Elster, Jon. 1979. *Ulysses and the Sirens: Studies in Rationality and Irrationality*. Cambridge: Cambridge University Press.

Ersner-Hershfield, Hal, M. Tess Garton, Kacey Ballard, Gregory R. Samanez-Larkin, and Brian Knutson. 2009a. "Don't Stop Thinking About Tomorrow: Individual Differences in Future Self-Continuity Account for Saving." *Judgment and Decision Making* 4 (4): 280–86.

Ersner-Hershfield, Hal, G. Elliott Wimmer, and Brian Knutson. 2009b. "Saving for the Future Self: Neural Measures of Future Self-Continuity Predict Temporal

Discounting." *Social Cognitive and Affective Neuroscience* 4 (1): 85–92. https://doi.org/10.1093/scan/nsn042.

Fuhrman, Joel. 2018. "The Hidden Dangers of Fast and Processed Food." *American Journal of Lifestyle Medicine* 12 (5): 375–81. https://doi.org/10.1177/1559827618766483.

Fujita, Kentaro. 2011. "On Conceptualizing Self-Control as More Than the Effortful Inhibition of Impulses." *Personality and Social Psychology Review* 15 (4): 352–66. https://doi.org/10.1177/1088868311411165.

Fujita, Kentaro, and H. Anna Han. 2009. "Moving Beyond Deliberative Control of Impulses." *Psychological Science* 20 (7): 799–804. https://doi.org/10.1111/j.1467-9280.2009.02372.x.

Fujita, Kentaro, Yaacov Trope, Nira Liberman, and Maya Levin-Sagi. 2006. "Construal Levels and Self-Control." *Journal of Personality and Social Psychology* 90 (3): 351–67. https://doi.org/10.1037/0022-3514.90.3.351.

Galinsky, Adam D., and Gordon B. Moskowitz. 2000. "Perspective-Taking: Decreasing Stereotype Expression, Stereotype Accessibility, and In-Group Favoritism." *Journal of Personality and Social Psychology* 78 (4): 708–24. https://doi.org/10.1037/0022-3514.78.4.708.

Geng, Joy J., and Simone Vossel. 2013. "Re-Evaluating the Role of TPJ in Attentional Control: Contextual Updating?" *Neuroscience and Biobehavioral Reviews*. Pergamon. https://doi.org/10.1016/j.neubiorev.2013.08.010.

Gilbert, Daniel T., and Timothy D. Wilson. 2007. "Prospection: Experiencing the Future." *Science* 317 (5843): 1351–54. https://doi.org/10.1126/science.1144161.

Hare, Todd A., Colin F. Camerer, and Antonio Rangel. 2009. "Self-Control in Decision-Making Involves Modulation of the VmPFC Valuation System." *Science* 324 (5927): 646–48. https://doi.org/10.1126/science.1168450.

Hare, Todd A., Jonathan Malmaud, and Antonio Rangel. 2011. "Focusing Attention on the Health Aspects of Foods Changes Value Signals in VmPFC and Improves Dietary Choice." *The Journal of Neuroscience* 31 (30): 11077–87. https://doi.org/10.1523/JNEUROSCI.6383-10.2011.

Hatfield, Elaine, John T. Cacioppo, and Richard L. Rapson. 1992. "Primitive Emotional Contagion." In *Review of Personality and Social Psychology: Vol. 14. Emotions and Social Behavior*, edited by M. S. Clark. Newbury Park: Sage.

Heider, Fritz. 1958. *The Psychology of Interpersonal Relations*. Hillsdale: Lawrence Erlbaum Associate.

Hein, Grit, Giorgia Silani, Kerstin Preuschoff, C. Daniel Batson, and Tania Singer. 2010. "Neural Responses to Ingroup and Outgroup Members' Suffering Predict Individual Differences in Costly Helping." *Neuron* 68 (1): 149–60. https://doi.org/10.1016/J.NEURON.2010.09.003.

Hershfield, Hal E. 2011. "Future Self-Continuity: How Conceptions of the Future Self Transform Intertemporal Choice." *Annals of the New York Academy of Sciences* 1235: 30–43. https://doi.org/10.1111/j.1749-6632.2011.06201.x.

———. 2019. "The Self over Time." *Current Opinion in Psychology* 26: 72–75. https://doi.org/10.1016/j.copsyc.2018.06.004.

Hershfield, Hal E., and Daniel M. Bartels. 2018. "The Future Self." In *The Psychology of Thinking About the Future*, edited by G. Oettingen, A. T. Sevincer, and P. Gollwitzer. New York: Guilford Press.

Hershfield, Hal E., Taya R. Cohen, and Leigh Thompson. 2012. "Short Horizons and Tempting Situations: Lack of Continuity to Our Future Selves Leads to Unethical Decision Making and Behavior." *Organizational Behavior and Human Decision Processes* 117 (2): 298–310. https://doi.org/10.1016/j.obhdp.2011.11.002.

Hershfield, Hal E., Daniel G. Goldstein, William F. Sharpe, Jesse Fox, Leo Yeykelis, Laura L. Carstensen, and Jeremy N. Bailenson. 2011. "Increasing Saving Behavior Through Age-Progressed Renderings of the Future Self." *Journal of Marketing Research* 48: S23–S37. https://doi.org/10.1509/jmkr.48.SPL.S23.

Holton, Richard. 1999. "Intention and Weakness of Will." *The Journal of Philosophy* 96 (5): 241–62. https://doi.org/10.2307/2564667.

Igelström, Kajsa M., and Michael S. A. Graziano. 2017. "The Inferior Parietal Lobule and Temporoparietal Junction: A Network Perspective." *Neuropsychologia* 105 (October): 70–83. https://doi.org/10.1016/J.NEUROPSYCHOLOGIA.2017.01.001.

Jackson, Philip L., Eric Brunet, Andrew N. Meltzoff, and Jean Decety. 2006. "Empathy Examined through the Neural Mechanisms Involved in Imagining How I Feel versus How You Feel Pain." *Neuropsychologia* 44 (5): 752–61. https://doi.org/10.1016/j.neuropsychologia.2005.07.015.

Jenkins, Adrianna C., and Ming Hsu. 2017. "Dissociable Contributions of Imagination and Willpower to the Malleability of Human Patience." *Psychological Science* 28 (7): 894–906. https://doi.org/10.1177/0956797617698133.

Jenkins, Adrianna C., C. Neil Macrae, and Jason P. Mitchell. 2008. "Repetition Suppression of Ventromedial Prefrontal Activity During Judgments of Self and Others." *Proceedings of the National Academy of Sciences of the United States of America* 105 (11): 4507–12. https://doi.org/10.1073/pnas.0708785105.

Jones, Edward E., and Richard E. Nisbett. 1972. "The Actor and the Observer: Divergent Perceptions of the Causes of Behavior." In *Attribution: Perceiving the Causes of Behavior*, edited by E. E. Jones, D. E. Kanouse, H. H. Kelley, R. E. Nisbett, S. Valins, and B. Weiner. Hillsdale: Lawrence Erlbaum Associates.

Kim, B. Kyu, and Gal Zauberman. 2019. "Psychological Time and Intertemporal Preference." *Current Opinion in Psychology*. https://doi.org/10.1016/j.copsyc.2018.06.005.

Kim, Hyunji, Simone Schnall, and Mathew P. White. 2013. "Similar Psychological Distance Reduces Temporal Discounting." *Personality and Social Psychology Bulletin* 39 (8): 1005–16. https://doi.org/10.1177/0146167213488214.

Krall, S. C., C. Rottschy, E. Oberwelland, D. Bzdok, P. T. Fox, S. B. Eickhoff, G. R. Fink, and K. Konrad. 2015. "The Role of the Right Temporoparietal Junction in Attention and Social Interaction as Revealed by ALE Meta-Analysis." *Brain Structure and Function* 220 (2): 587–604. https://doi.org/10.1007/s00429-014-0803-z.

Lamm, Claus, C. Daniel Batson, and Jean Decety. 2007. "The Neural Substrate of Human Empathy: Effects of Perspective-Taking and Cognitive Appraisal."

Journal of Cognitive Neuroscience 19 (1): 42–58. https://doi.org/10.1162/jocn.2007.19.1.42.

Laran, Juliano, and Chris Janiszewski. 2011. "Work or Fun? How Task Construal and Completion Influence Regulatory Behavior." *Journal of Consumer Research* 37 (6): 967–83. https://doi.org/10.1086/656576.

Lewis, Neil A., and Daphna Oyserman. 2015. "When Does the Future Begin? Time Metrics Matter, Connecting Present and Future Selves." *Psychological Science* 26 (6): 816–25. https://doi.org/10.1177/0956797615572231.

Liberman, Nira, and Yaacov Trope. 2003. "Construal Level Theory of Intertemporal Judgment and Decision." In *Time and Decision: Economic and Psychological Perspectives of Intertemporal Choice*, edited by G. Loewenstein, D. Read, and R. Baumeister. New York: Russell Sage Foundation.

Loewenstein, George. 1996. "Out of Control: Visceral Influence on Behavior." *Organizational Behavior and Human Decision Processes* 65 (3): 272–92.

———. 2000. "Emotions in Economic Theory and Economic Behavior." *American Economic Review* 90 (2): 426–32. https://doi.org/10.1257/aer.90.2.426.

Loewenstein, George, Ted O'Donoghue, and Matthew Rabin. 2003. "Projection Bias in Predicting Future Utility." *Quarterly Journal of Economics* 118 (4): 1209–48. https://doi.org/10.1162/003355303322552784.

Loewenstein, George, Drazen Prelec, and Catherine Shatto. 1998. "Hot/Cold Intrapersonal Empathy Gaps and the under-Prediction of Curiosity." *Unpublished*.

Malkoc, Selin A., Gal Zauberman, and James R. Bettman. 2010. "Unstuck from the Concrete: Carryover Effects of Abstract Mindsets in Intertemporal Preferences." *Organizational Behavior and Human Decision Processes* 113 (2): 112–26. https://doi.org/10.1016/J.OBHDP.2010.07.003.

Mazar, Nina, On Amir, and Dan Ariely. 2008. "The Dishonesty of Honest People: A Theory of Self-Concept Maintenance." *Journal of Marketing Research* 45 (6): 633–44.

McCarroll, Christopher Jude, and Erica Cosentino. 2020. "Rewarding One's Future Self: Psychological Connectedness, Episodic Prospection, and a Puzzle about Perspective." *Review of Philosophy and Psychology*: 1–19. https://doi.org/10.1007/s13164-020-00460-2.

McCrea, Sean M., Frank Wieber, and Andrea L. Myers. 2012. "Construal Level Mind-Sets Moderate Self- and Social Stereotyping." *Journal of Personality and Social Psychology* 102 (1): 51–68. https://doi.org/10.1037/a0026108.

Mele, Alfred R. 1987. *Irrationality: An Essay on Akrasia, Self-Deception, and Self-Control*. New York: Oxford University Press. https://doi.org/10.2307/2185521.

Meyer, Meghan L., Carrie L. Masten, Yina Ma, Chenbo Wang, Zhenhao Shi, Naomi I. Eisenberger, and Shihui Han. 2013. "Empathy for the Social Suffering of Friends and Strangers Recruits Distinct Patterns of Brain Activation." *Social Cognitive and Affective Neuroscience* 8 (4): 446–54. https://doi.org/10.1093/scan/nss019.

Miller, Dale T., Julie S. Downs, and Deborah A. Prentice. 1998. "Minimal Conditions for the Creation of a Unit Relationship: The Social Bond between Birthdaymates." *European Journal of Social Psychology* 28 (3): 475–81. https://doi.org/10.1002/(SICI)1099-0992(199805/06)28:3<475::AID-EJSP881>3.0.CO;2-M.

Mischel, Walter. 1974. "Processes in Delay of Gratification." *Advances in Experimental Social Psychology* 7 (C): 249–92. https://doi.org/10.1016/S0065-2601(08)60039-8.

Mischel, Walter, Yuichi Shoda, and Monica L. Rodriguez. 1989. "Delay of Gratification in Children." *Science* 244 (4907): 933–38. https://doi.org/10.1126/science.2658056.

Mitchell, Jason P., Jessica Schirmer, Daniel L. Ames, and Daniel T. Gilbert. 2011. "Medial Prefrontal Cortex Predicts Intertemporal Choice." *Journal of Cognitive Neuroscience* 23 (4): 857–66. https://doi.org/10.1162/jocn.2010.21479.

Molouki, Sarah, and Daniel M. Bartels. 2020. "Are Future Selves Treated Like Others? Comparing Determinants and Levels of Intrapersonal and Interpersonal Allocations." *Cognition* 196: 1–10. https://doi.org/10.1016/j.cognition.2019.104150.

Nussbaum, Shiri, Yaacov Trope, and Nira Liberman. 2003. "Creeping Dispositionism: The Temporal Dynamics of Behavior Prediction." *Journal of Personality and Social Psychology* 84 (3): 485–97. https://doi.org/10.1037/0022-3514.84.3.485.

O'Connell, Garret, Anastasia Christakou, and Bhismadev Chakrabarti. 2015. "The Role of Simulation in Intertemporal Choices." *Frontiers in Neuroscience* 9 (94): 1–10. https://doi.org/10.3389/fnins.2015.00094.

O'Connell, Garret, Chun-Ting Hsu, Anastasia Christakou, and Bhismadev Chakrabarti. 2018. "Thinking About Others and the Future: Neural Correlates of Perspective Taking Relate to Preferences for Delayed Rewards." *Cognitive, Affective, & Behavioral Neuroscience* 18 (1): 35–42. https://doi.org/10.3758/s13415-017-0550-8.

Ochsner, Kevin N., Jennifer A. Silvers, and Jason T. Buhle. 2012. "Functional Imaging Studies of Emotion Regulation: A Synthetic Review and Evolving Model of the Cognitive Control of Emotion." *Annals of the New York Academy of Sciences* 1251: E1–E24. https://doi.org/10.1111/j.1749-6632.2012.06751.x.

Palombo, Daniela J., Margaret M. Keane, and Mieke Verfaellie. 2015. "The Medial Temporal Lobes are Critical for Reward-Based Decision Making under Conditions that Promote Episodic Future Thinking." *Hippocampus* 25 (3): 345–53. https://doi.org/10.1002/hipo.22376.

Parfit, Derek. 1971. "Personal Identity." *The Philosophical Review* 80 (1): 3–27. https://doi.org/10.1007/s11017-010-9147-8.

———. 1984. *Reasons and Persons*. Oxford: Clarendon Press.

Peters, Jan, and Christian Büchel. 2010. "Episodic Future Thinking Reduces Reward Delay Discounting through an Enhancement of Prefrontal-Mediotemporal Interactions." *Neuron* 66 (1): 138–48. https://doi.org/10.1016/j.neuron.2010.03.026.

Pronin, Emily, Christopher Y. Olivola, and Kathleen A. Kennedy. 2008. "Doing Unto Future Selves As You Would Do Unto Others: Psychological Distance and Decision Making." *Personality and Social Psychology Bulletin* 34 (2): 224–36. https://doi.org/10.1177/0146167207310023.

Pronin, Emily, and Lee Ross. 2006. "Temporal Differences in Trait Self-Ascription: When the Self is Seen as an Other." *Journal of Personality and Social Psychology* 90 (2): 197–209. https://doi.org/10.1037/0022-3514.90.2.197.

Rangel, Antonio, and John A. Clithero. 2014. "The Computation of Stimulus Values in Simple Choice." In *Neuroeconomics: Decision Making and the Brain*, edited by P. W. Glimcher and E. Fehr, 2nd ed. London: Academic Press. https://doi.org/10.1016/B978-0-12-416008-8.00008-5.

Read, Daniel, Shane Frederick, Burcu Orsel, and Juwaria Rahman. 2005. "Four Score and Seven Years From Now: The Date/Delay Effect in Temporal Discounting." *Management Science* 51 (9): 1326–35. https://doi.org/10.1287/mnsc.1050.0412.

Read, Daniel, Christopher Y. Olivola, and David J. Hardisty. 2017. "The Value of Nothing: Asymmetric Attention to Opportunity Costs Drives Intertemporal Decision Making." *Management Science* 63 (12): 4277–97. https://doi.org/10.1287/mnsc.2016.2547.

Savitsky, Kenneth, Boaz Keysar, Nicholas Epley, Travis Carter, and Ashley Swanson. 2011. "The Closeness-Communication Bias: Increased Egocentrism among Friends Versus Strangers." *Journal of Experimental Social Psychology* 47 (1): 269–73. https://doi.org/10.1016/J.JESP.2010.09.005.

Schacter, Daniel L., Roland G. Benoit, and Karl K. Szpunar. 2017. "Episodic Future Thinking: Mechanisms and Functions." *Current Opinion in Behavioral Sciences* 17: 41–50. https://doi.org/10.1016/J.COBEHA.2017.06.002.

Schelling, Thomas C. 1984. "Self-Command in Practice, in Policy, and in a Theory of Rational Choice." *The American Economic Review* 74: 1–11.

Schurz, Matthias, Joaquim Radua, Markus Aichhorn, Fabio Richlan, and Josef Perner. 2014. "Fractionating Theory of Mind: A Meta-Analysis of Functional Brain Imaging Studies." *Neuroscience and Biobehavioral Reviews* 42: 9–34. https://doi.org/10.1016/j.neubiorev.2014.01.009.

Shanton, Karen, and Alvin Goldman. 2010. "Simulation Theory." *Wiley Interdisciplinary Reviews: Cognitive Science* 1 (4): 527–38. https://doi.org/10.1002/wcs.33.

Singer, Tania, and Anita Tusche. 2014. "Understanding Others: Brain Mechanisms of Theory of Mind and Empathy." In *Neuroeconomics: Decision Making and the Brain*, edited by P. W. Glimcher and E. Fehr, 2nd ed. London: Academic Press. https://doi.org/10.1016/B978-0-12-416008-8.00027-9.

Soutschek, Alexander, Marius Moisa, Christian C. Ruff, and Philippe N. Tobler. 2020. "The Right Temporoparietal Junction Enables Delay of Gratification by Allowing Decision Makers to Focus on Future Events." *PLoS Biology* 18 (8): e3000800. https://doi.org/10.1371/JOURNAL.PBIO.3000800.

Soutschek, Alexander, Christian C. Ruff, Tina Strombach, Tobias Kalenscher, and Philippe N. Tobler. 2016. "Brain Stimulation Reveals Crucial Role of Overcoming Self-Centeredness in Self-Control." *Science Advances* 2 (10): e1600992.

Spreng, R. Nathan, and Cheryl L. Grady. 2010. "Patterns of Brain Activity Supporting Autobiographical Memory, Prospection, and Theory of Mind, and Their Relationship to the Default Mode Network." *Journal of Cognitive Neuroscience* 22 (6): 1112–23. https://doi.org/10.1162/jocn.2009.21282.

Spreng, R. Nathan, Raymond A. Mar, and Alice S. N. Kim. 2009. "The Common Neural Basis of Autobiographical Memory, Prospection, Navigation, Theory of Mind, and the Default Mode: A Quantitative Meta-Analysis." *Journal of Cognitive Neuroscience* 21 (3): 489–510. https://doi.org/10.1162/jocn.2008.21029.

Stotland, Ezra. 1969. "Exploratory Investigations of Empathy." *Advances in Experimental Social Psychology* 4 (C): 271–314. https://doi.org/10.1016/S0065-2601(08)60080-5.

Suddendorf, Thomas, and Michael C. Corballis. 1997. "Mental Time Travel and the Evolution of the Human Mind." *Genetic, Social, and General Psychology Monographs* 123 (2): 133–67.

———. 2007. "The Evolution of Foresight: What Is Mental Time Travel, and is it Unique to Humans?" *The Behavioral and Brain Sciences* 30 (3): 299–313. https://doi.org/10.1017/S0140525X07001975.

Tamir, Diana I., and Jason P. Mitchell. 2013. "Anchoring and Adjustment during Social Inferences." *Journal of Experimental Psychology: General* 142 (1): 151–62. https://doi.org/10.1037/a0028232.

Thaler, Richard H., and H. M. Shefrin. 1981. "An Economic Theory of Self-Control." *Journal of Political Economy* 89 (2): 392–406. https://doi.org/10.2307/1833317.

Trope, Yaacov, and Nira Liberman. 2000. "Temporal Construal and Time-Dependent Changes in Preference." *Journal of Personality and Social Psychology* 79 (6): 876–89.

———. 2003. "Temporal Construal." *Psychological Review* 110 (3): 403–21.

———. 2010. "Construal-Level Theory of Psychological Distance." *Psychological Review* 117 (2): 440–63. https://doi.org/10.1037/a0018963.

Tulving, E. 1985. "Memory and Consciousness." *Canadian Psychology* 26 (1): 1–12. https://doi.org/10.1037/h0080017.

Viganò, Eleonora. 2017. "Adam Smith's Theory of Prudence Updated With Neuroscientific and Behavioral Evidence." *Neuroethics* 10 (2): 215–33. https://doi.org/10.1007/s12152-017-9332-9.

Wilson, Timothy D., and Daniel T. Gilbert. 2003. "Affective Forecasting." *Advances in Experimental Social Psychology* 35: 345–411. https://doi.org/10.1016/S0065-2601(03)01006-2.

———. 2005. "Affective Forecasting: Knowing What to Want." *Current Directions in Psychological Science* 14 (3): 131–34. https://doi.org/10.1111/j.0963-7214.2005.00355.x.

World Health Organization. 2013. "Global Action Plan for the Prevention and Control of Noncommunicable Diseases 2013–2020." https://doi.org/978 92 4 1506236.

Xu, Xiaojing, Xiangyu Zuo, Xiaoying Wang, and Shihui Han. 2009. "Do You Feel My Pain? Racial Group Membership Modulates Empathic Neural Responses." *The Journal of Neuroscience* 29 (26): 8525–29. https://doi.org/10.1523/JNEUROSCI.2418-09.2009.

Yi, Richard, Allison Stuppy-Sullivan, Alison Pickover, and Reid D. Landes. 2017. "Impact of Construal Level Manipulations on Delay Discounting." *PLoS One* 12 (5): e0177240. https://doi.org/10.1371/journal.pone.0177240.

2 What is the nature of the relationship in which we stand with our future selves? Practical and moral issues of one's perception of the future self

1. Introduction

In the first chapter, I dealt with ICs: decisions involving a trade-off between the magnitude of the choice outcome and the time at which the outcome is received. These choices are a simplified version of the kind of decisions I address in this chapter: *diachronic self-regarding decisions*. These are decisions that involve the individual making them, rather than other individuals, and have consequences for her later self. They are called *self-regarding* because they concern one's relationship with oneself, and *diachronic* because they involve one's earlier and later selves.

Self-regarding decisions comprise two normative elements: *prudence* and *authenticity*. I conceive of prudence as the care for oneself aiming to one's good life, also termed well-being in philosophy.[1] While much philosophical literature to date has focused on the well-being aspect of prudence, in this and the following chapter, I will focus on care for oneself in terms of protecting one's future agency, namely, the future self's capacity to be an agent. In moral philosophy, one's relationship with—and thus care for—herself has been less studied than one's relationship with others, as morality from Kant onwards has been mainly interpreted as interpersonal (i.e., regulating the relationships among persons) and other-regarding (i.e., concerning not one's own but other individuals' good) (Annas 1995; Den Uyl 1991, chs. 1, 6). Authenticity is the capacity to live according to ideals that the agent reflectively and sincerely accepts at the time of action (Brink 2003, 215, 227).

I focus on diachronic self-regarding decisions whose stake is something relevant to and valuable for the individual. An example of a high-stakes diachronic self-regarding decision (henceforth, "diachronic self-regarding decision") is the choice between dedicating oneself to a career and dedicating oneself to raising a family in cases where the two options cannot be reconciled in one life (i.e., the individual can choose one, but not both).

DOI: 10.4324/9781003122142-3

Another example is the choice to move to another country to seek more and better life opportunities in an unfamiliar environment versus to stay in one's home country, which is a familiar environment but has fewer life opportunities.

I focus on diachronic self-regarding decisions involving the individual's present and future selves because the aim of my Moral Theory of Prudence in the next chapter is to guide the individual when she faces a diachronic self-regarding decision. Certainly, each diachronic decision between the present and future selves becomes a diachronic decision between the past and present selves at a certain point in time and—when more time has passed—between two past selves. However, after such a decision has been made, the individual cannot change it, and thus my moral theory cannot guide her. The exact temporal distance between one's present and future selves depends on the diachronic self-regarding decision in question and its effects, and thus cannot be specified once for all cases.

Diachronic self-regarding decisions are challenging for the individual facing them for two reasons. First, when the individual makes the decision, she does not and cannot know whether she will agree with the decision at a later time. In fact, the preferences, values, projects, and character of the individual in the future (or, we can say, of the individual's future self) are not yet known. They might be similar to those of the individual in the present, but this is not necessarily the case, since the individual could undergo a significant change at a later time. Moreover, the individual's later self may not come to exist at all because of, for instance, a fatal accident. Second, diachronic self-regarding decisions are challenging because, although they will affect the individual at a later time, the individual's later self cannot have a say in the decision made by the individual's earlier self, who must decide for both.

Considering that the individual may change at a later time and that individuals tend to discount their future utilities (as seen in Chapter 1), the individual at the present time and the individual at a later time may disagree on the best course of action to take in several diachronic self-regarding decisions. In such cases, the diachronic self-regarding decisions are *diachronic self-regarding conflicts of values* (henceforth, "diachronic self-regarding conflicts").[2] Diachronic self-regarding conflicts are choices in which what we take care of and consider the right thing to do at present opposes that which we will take care of and consider the right thing to do in the future. Whether a diachronic self-regarding decision is a diachronic self-regarding conflict can be determined after the decision is made and its effects on the individual's future self have occurred. Before this point, while the individual may expect that her future self will disagree with the decision, she cannot be sure.

40 Our relationship with our future selves

The aim of this chapter is to analyze our relationships with our future selves, which requires tackling two topics: one's care for oneself (i.e., prudence) and the identity relation between an individual's present and future selves. First, I discuss the main views on the morality of prudence in moral philosophy and contend that prudence is a moral requirement. Second, I outline a minimal, realistic model of practical identity that supports the interpretation of diachronic self-regarding decisions as decisions between two agents. Third, I identify the moral features of the present-self–future-self relationship and, on that basis, I propose a new interpretation of diachronic self-regarding decisions as part of *intergenerational ethics*: I argue that they can be understood as a special case of the relationship between contemporary people and future generations. The conception of prudence as moral, the minimal, realistic model of the agent, and the four moral features provide the theoretical basis for the next chapter's elaboration of a moral theory of prudence, which regulates the relationship between the individual's earlier and later selves in diachronic self-regarding decisions.

2. The morality of prudence

In this section, I give an overview of the main positions on the morality of prudence, with a focus on the contemporary authors who have dealt with prudence in the context of diachronic self-regarding decisions. I then take the first step toward defending the thesis that prudence is a moral requirement—namely, that prudent acts are morally right and required. I do not provide an exhaustive account of the positions on the relationship between prudence and morality because such an account would take the chapter off topic.[3] For the same reason, I do not deal with the topics of practical reasoning involving prudence, such as the requirements of rationality[4] (except for temporal neutrality; see section 2.1), and the metaethical issues of prudence, such as the transmission of the influence of prudential reasons over time.[5]

2.1 Ancient and modern views on prudence

In everyday language, morality is commonly understood as regulating the relationship between the individual and others (Neblett 1969, 71; Timmermann 2006, 505), and being moral can be read as having other-regarding goals (Schmidtz 1997, 107). In this common understanding of morality, one's relationship with oneself (and thus the present-self–future-self relationship) is neither relevant to nor part of morality. This clear-cut distinction between prudence and morality has its roots in modern ethics (which started with Kant), was already assumed as axiomatic by Sidgwick (1962

[1874], 496–509), and nowadays is adopted by all major families of moral theories.

The modern distinction between prudence and morality contrasts with the position of ancient ethical theories, which focused on providing the agent with a clear, articulated, and correct account of her final end (i.e., happiness) and how best to achieve it (i.e., how to live a good life) (Annas 1995, 241, 245; Irwin 1995). In Aristotle, prudence—also termed *practical wisdom*—is the intellectual excellence that enables one to deliberate well about the things that are generally conducive to the good life (Aristotle 2000, 1140a25–28). In the ancient ethical framework, prudential reasoning and moral reasoning are not distinct, and prudence is the care for one's own good. Here, "good" is conceived not as self-interest but as self-perfection (Annas 1995, 244). One's own good is the first order of concern of ancient ethics (Den Uyl 1991, 5, 20).

In modern ethics, the first order of concern is the individual's relation with others (Den Uyl 1991, 42). In this framework, prudence is considered a self-interested behavior that consists of seeking one's own overall happiness or well-being. According to Kant, prudence is not moral, as people naturally seek their present and future happiness. Rather, prudence is only rational: it is the use of the best means to achieve one's own happiness (Kant 2006 [1785], 4:416: 27; Den Uyl 1991, ch. 6).[6] Furthermore, one's relationship with oneself is not usually considered in modern moral theories because of the influence of liberalism and the preeminence that it attributes to autonomy. In the liberal tradition, since the individual is an autonomous being, her actions are always morally permissible, if their effects will be on herself (Mill 2003 [1859], chs. 4–5).

In the modern view of prudence (henceforth, the *standard view*), prudence is normative according to the requirements of rationality, not morality. I focus on the requirement of rationality that is relevant to the discussion of diachronic self-regarding decisions: *temporal neutrality*. This is the thesis that a difference in *when* something happens is not a difference in its value (i.e., in *how desirable* that something is). Thus, temporal neutrality requires that the prudent agent should have equal concern for all parts of her life, as the temporal location of benefits and harms in her life has no intrinsic significance (Sidgwick 1962 [1874], 381). In an IC in which there is a similar degree of uncertainty with regard to obtaining either the sooner smaller or the later larger reward, temporal neutrality requires the sacrifice of the present gratification for the greater reward in the future. Namely, it demands choosing the later larger reward. From the perspective of temporal neutrality, favoring one's own near-term interests over long-term ones is a failure of rationality.

42 *Our relationship with our future selves*

Adam Smith's concept of prudence was an exception in modern ethics, as he considers prudence to be moral (Smith 1976 [1790], VI.i.1–12: 212–15; Den Uyl 1991, ch. 5).[7] In Smith's moral system, prudence is the virtue of appropriate care for oneself: it is self-centered because its objects are one's own personal interests and well-being (1976 [1790], VI.i.5: 213), but it is open to the care of others in that it is restrained by the sense of justice and supported by self-command (Smith 1976 [1790], VI.iii.1: 237; Viganò 2017). The sense of justice does not allow the individual to care for herself at the expense of others (Smith 1976 [1790], II.iii.1.5: 95–96). Self-command is the ability to exercise discipline over one's desire for present enjoyments in favor of probable greater pleasure in the future and to curb selfish passions to a level that can be approved intersubjectively (Smith 1976 [1790], VI.i.11: 215; VI.iii.1: 237).

2.2 Contemporary views on prudence

In this section, I present the conceptions of prudence in the contemporary approaches to diachronic self-regarding decisions. I discuss how they propose solving diachronic self-regarding decisions in the next chapter.

Parfit has opened the door for abandoning the axiomatic distinction between morality and prudence by contending that great imprudence is morally wrong (Parfit 1984, 318–19). However, he discusses only the immorality of great acts of imprudence, but not the morality of prudence. Parfit seeks a moral justification of prudence that is not based on the traditional philosophical views of prudence as a natural tendency, and personal identity as temporally extended to the duration of one's life. This is because his view of personal identity undermines both assumptions.[8]

In Parfit's approach to personal identity, *psychological connectedness* is the holding of direct psychological connections in terms of memories, intentions, beliefs, and desires, which occurs in consecutive phases of one's life. *Psychological continuity* is the holding of overlapping chains of direct psychological connections, which takes place between nonconsecutive phases of one's life (Parfit 1971, 20, 1984, 205). In Parfit's account, if a person, say Claire, has most of the memories, intentions, beliefs, and desires at time t that she will have 20 years later ($t + 20\,y$), then Claire at t and Claire at $t + 20\,y$ are the same person because Claire at t shares psychological states with Claire at $t + 20\,y$. If Claire at $t + 20\,y$ has different memories, values, intentions, beliefs, and desires than Claire at t, then Claire at t and Claire at $t + 20\,y$ are two numerically different persons. According to Parfit, psychological continuity is influenced by time (Parfit 1984, 312) in the sense that it is more likely that the psychological continuity between two stages of a person's life that are close to one another in time (e.g., 30-year-old Claire and

35-year-old Claire) is higher than that between two stages that are far to one another (e.g., 30-year-old Claire and 65-year-old Claire). Parfit defines the relation of psychological continuity or connectedness as *relation R* (Parfit 1984, 214).

If the traditional view on personal identity is rejected, as in Parfit's approach, it may seem that we have no reason to take special concern or care for our future selves because, from a moral perspective, the individual is no more obliged to take care of her future self than to take care of other people (Parfit 1984, 306–7). Yet, according to Parfit, relation *R* between one's earlier and later selves is a sufficient reason for paying special concern to one's future self (Parfit 1984, 312). Parfit defends the moral legitimacy of a discount rate of one's future utilities on the basis of the weakening of one's relation *R* (Parfit 1984, 313). Such a discount rate undermines temporal neutrality (Parfit 1984, 314), as the individual cares more for the parts of her life that are more psychologically continuous or connected.

Parfit proposes justifying the immorality of great imprudence by extending the sphere of action covered by morality and suggests two strategies for doing so (Parfit 1984, 318). The first is grounding the care for oneself in an agent-neutral principle of beneficence: acts of great imprudence are wrong because they increase the sum of suffering in the world (Parfit 1984, 318). In this strategy, the justification for the immorality of great imprudence is consequentialist, and the care for our future selves becomes a sort of impersonal duty that applies when the present self intends to take an action that will have seriously negative consequences for the future self—for example, a child taking up smoking (Parfit 1984, 319). The second strategy for justifying the immorality of great imprudence involves extending the *agent-relative* part of a moral theory.[9] Among the special obligations descending from the relationships in which we stand with some individuals (e.g., parents, fellow citizens, customers), Parfit proposes including the special obligation descending from our relationship with our future selves. Such an obligation consists of caring for our future selves (Parfit 1984, 318).[10]

Unlike Parfit, many contributions to the debate on prudence deal with the rationality of prudence but not its morality (e.g., Nagel 1970; Brink 2003, 2011; Cureton 2016; Bruckner 2003), as does the standard view of prudence. The recent approaches to diachronic self-regarding decisions mainly conceive prudent actions as those that are best for the agent with respect to her whole life and take into account the fact that the agent may change her values throughout her life. Accordingly, most of these approaches identify a stable and general standpoint from which to assess prudent actions: the idealized agent (Cureton 2016; Brink 2003; Pettigrew 2020; McKerlie 2007; Dorsey 2021).[11]

In contrast with the standard view, Arvan (2020) proposes considering a reconceptualizing of morality as reducing to prudence (Arvan 2020, 132). He conceives of prudence as acting in ways that have the best expected lifetime utility for the agent (Arvan 2020, 26–28). According to Arvan, prudence is founded on individuals' internalizations of moral risk aversion, which lead them to avoid violating moral norms and prefer behaving morally for its own sake. Because of the radical uncertainty of agents' lives and the empirical regularity with which moral violations tend to be caught and punished, Arvan contends that prudent behavior requires one to behave morally. He holds that the agent has learned since childhood that moral behavior has greater expected lifetime benefits than immoral behavior. Furthermore, immoral behavior is more regrettable than moral behavior due to the former's negative consequences (Arvan 2020, ch. 2). According to Arvan, morally risk-averse agents learn to care about their past and future because doing so usually brings about the best expected lifetime outcome (Arvan 2020, 45, 51). Caring for the future includes, in this theory, avoiding potential future regret (Arvan 2020, 51). For Arvan, the best strategy for avoiding possible regret is to follow the *Categorical-Instrumental Imperative*. The latter requires the individual to act on voluntary (i.e., chosen) interests upon which all of an individual's selves agree, regardless of how the past and future might turn out and what interests the past, present, and future selves could possibly have (Arvan 2020, 63–64). According to Arvan, as an individual's possible future self may care about the interests of other human and nonhuman sentient beings, an agreement among all of an individual's possible selves must include the interests in other human and nonhuman sentient beings (Arvan 2020, 64–65). The Categorical-Instrumental Imperative is a requirement of prudence that demands agreement among all of an individual's selves. Therefore, Arvan contends that the Categorical-Instrumental Imperative is the basis of moral normativity—that is, the requirement to justify one's actions to other human and nonhuman sentient beings (Arvan 2020, 4, 87). For this reason, he proposes reducing morality to prudence (Arvan 2020, 132).

2.3 My view: What empirical findings tell us about prudence and the first step toward defending the morality of prudence

Temporal neutrality requires sacrificing present gratification for a greater reward in the future. By combining temporal neutrality with the widespread philosophical view contending that the time slices of an individual's life are not independent but form part of one unit,[12] it follows that, in an IC, preferring a later larger outcome over a sooner smaller one is not a sacrifice. In this view, from the agent's perspective, such a choice feels like a delayed gratification because the agent that makes the sacrifice is the same that will receive the benefits of that sacrifice (Brink 2003, 223–25; Crisp 2017; Rawls 1999, 21, 259). However, according to Scanlon (1998, 127), from the agent's perspective, her sacrifice of her present well-being for the sake of her future well-being resembles giving up part of her well-being for the sake of a family member or friend.

The neurobehavioral studies presented in the previous chapter support Scanlon's contention. As seen, experimental subjects perceived their future selves as distinct from their present selves in tasks of trait ascription, visual imagery (Pronin and Ross 2006), and behavior explanation (Nussbaum et al. 2003). In addition, the brain areas activated in mentalizing about one's future selves are similar to those activated for mentalizing about other people and different from those activated when the subjects think about their present selves (Mitchell et al. 2011). Therefore, the typical (in the sense of real) individual taking action (i.e., the typical agent) does not necessarily perceives herself as temporally extended in the future. The real agent is similar to Strawson's *episodic agent*: an agent who takes care of herself for a period of time shorter than the person's life of which she is part (Strawson 2004, 431).

In Chapter 1, I also showed that, in laboratory IC tasks, subjects usually assign more burdens (e.g., hours of voluntary work, quantity of a distasteful liquid to drink) to their future selves or to another person than to their present selves (Pronin et al. 2008). Moreover, there is ample evidence that, in real-world ICs, people adopt behaviors with long-term unhealthy consequences, such as overeating, and do not save enough for retirement (e.g., Chapman and Elstein 1995; Chapman 1996; Hausman 1979; Rasmussen et al. 2010). On the basis of these findings, I contend that, as favoring one's present self over one's future self harms the latter in the long run (e.g., obesity, poverty in later life), this behavior can be judged as morally wrong. Showing the immorality of imprudence on the basis of the harm that imprudent acts inflict on the individual's future self is my first step toward defending the thesis that prudence is a moral requirement. Parfit takes this step as well.[13] In section 3.4 and in the next chapter, I go somewhat further than Parfit. I contend that prudence is moral by showing that the definition of a moral agent implies care for oneself and that caring for oneself requires protecting one's future moral agency (i.e., the capacity to be a moral agent).[14] As I argue that prudence is moral, my account reconnects to the ancient view of prudence, in which care for oneself is considered moral.

3. Diachronic self-regarding decisions as decisions between two agents: Practical identity in diachronic self-regarding morality

Since I deal with prudence as care for oneself, I must specify what the entity defined as "oneself" is. Accordingly, I tackle the issue of personal identity in the present-self–future-self relationship in diachronic self-regarding decisions. In this section, I delineate a model of practical identity—the practical agent—that takes into account the typical behavior of individuals facing such decisions that has been observed in empirical studies. Then, based on the definition of a moral agent, I take a second step toward defending the thesis that prudence is a moral requirement.

3.1 Personal identity and practical identity

The relevant entities involved in the present-self–future-self relationship can be described on two levels. The first is metaphysical and regards the *metaphysical person*: a temporally extended being that, in the case of human persons, is located in the same body.[15] I do not deal with this level, as diachronic self-regarding decisions require only a practical agent (henceforth, agent), who is a subject able to deliberate, decide, and autonomously take actions for which she can provide reasons (Anscombe 1957; Davidson 1963; Frankfurt 1971; Mele 2003). The second level of description of the present-self–future-self relationship is practical and concerns the agent. As one needs only a practical conception of herself to be effective in the *practical sphere* (Korsgaard 1989, 110–11; Morton 2013, 812)—that is, the sphere of action—I focus on the second level of description and deal with the identity of the agent, to whom I refer as a *self*. A self is an agent situated at a temporal stage of the person and coexisting with the person. Such a self can be interpreted as a morally relevant attribute of the person but cannot be conceived of as an entity metaphysically distinct from the person.

A person's earlier and later selves are that person's diachronic selves. A person's diachronic selves are more connected to each other than the diachronic selves of two or more distinct persons. The reason is that the causal relation among a person's diachronic selves is stronger than the causal relations among the diachronic selves of two or more distinct persons because of two factors. First, the diachronic selves of a person are part of that person, while the diachronic selves of two persons belong to different persons. Second, every decision and action taken by one's self directly affects one's successive decisions and actions and thus one's successive self.

My definition of the self is close to Korsgaard's characterization of the unified agent as a practical and not metaphysical identity (Korsgaard 1989, 1996, 100–3, 229–33, 2009, 25). However, I do not subscribe to her idea that the principle of prudence should be a formal principle unifying the agent like Kant's Categorical Imperative (Korsgaard 2009, 52, 58).[16]

3.2 The minimal, realistic model of the agent

I identify three main elements that characterize a typical human agent. The first two elements derive from the definition of a practical agent, while the third derives from the studies on the perception of one's future self. These three elements are the components of a minimal, realistic model of a human practical agent and the basis of any realistic account of practical identity.

In moral philosophy, an agent is conceived as the principle of her voluntary actions, namely actions that she is motivated and has reasons to take, and that she freely initiates. The agent's reasons for action are personal commitments, ideals, projects, values, and the like she wants to pursue or realize. I define these as the agent's *set of normative principles of action*. The set of normative principles of action is the first component of the minimal, realistic model of the agent. An agent's set of normative principles characterizes her as that specific agent. I maintain that there are some normative principles about which the agent cares more and considers more important than other ones; I call the former *core normative principles of action*. In the case of conflicts among normative principles of action, the core principles prevail over less fundamental ones for the agent and motivate her action. I contend that when, in a person's life, the core normative principles change, an agent (i.e., the agent with the earlier set of core normative principles) ceases to exist in this person's life and another (i.e., the agent with the new set of core normative principles) enters into existence. In my account of the agent, core normative principles are the criterion of numerical identity of the agent or self, not of persons. Therefore, in my account, when person A changes her core normative principles, she does not become a numerically different person (i.e., she does not become person B). When person A changes her core normative principles, it means that she has a new agent (agent b), who is numerically different from the previous agent (agent a), who had the previous core normative principles. Both a and b are part of person A.

The second component of the minimal, realistic account follows from the first. Some of the agent's normative principles of action take time to be achieved, such as projects and long-term commitments. Therefore, they require an agent that is minimally extended over time and can thus pursue them. Similarly, Korsgaard contends that an essential characteristic of practical identity is planning ability, since agents express their identities in their projects, and that planning presupposes a temporally extended being (Korsgaard 1989, 2009, chs. 5, 9). The agent's minimal temporal extension is the second component of my model.

The third component of the minimal, realistic model of the agent is based on empirical evidence regarding subjects' behavior and thus applies to an account of practical identity in which the agent is a human being. As seen in Chapter 1, neurobehavioral studies show that the more the individual perceives her future self as similar to herself, the more she cares for her future self. To recall these studies, in ICs, when subjects perceived their future selves as similar to themselves, they sacrificed a present reward for a greater future one. When they perceived their later selves as different from themselves, they made decisions that favored their present selves over their future selves (Ersner-Hershfield et al. 2009; Hershfield et al. 2011; Pronin et al. 2008; Bartels and Urminsky 2011, 2015). A realistic model of the human agent should take into account the individual's perception that, if she feels weak or no psychological connection with her future self, favoring her future self over her present self does not feel like a compensation but a sacrifice for another individual, as Scanlon indicated (1998, 127).[17] Thus, the current agent's perceived connection with the successive agents that are part of the same person affects the current agent's care for the successive agents. The third component of a minimal account of practical identity is the dependence of the agent's care for the successive agents on her perceived connection with the successive agents. This component is close to Parfit's characterization of the person in terms of relation R, although he deals with metaphysical identity and not practical identity.

In sum, in my theory, the individual facing a diachronic self-regarding decision is a practical entity (i.e., a self) situated at a temporal stage of the metaphysical person and coexisting with her. The essential components of this practical entity are a set of normative principles that provide her with reasons for action, her extension over a certain period of time (which does not necessarily coincide with the person's life of which the agent is a part), and care for the future self depending on her perceived connection with that self.

3.3 The minimal, realistic agent in diachronic self-regarding decisions

In the widespread philosophical view of personal identity, a person's life is composed of time slices that are not independent entities. In contrast, my minimal, realistic account admits the possibility that two or more time slices of a person's life can be independent in the sense of distinct practical identities, even though they belong to the same person. This possibility gives a new reading of *personal transformative experiences*. Personal transformative experiences are events that change how someone experiences being who she is—that is, the experiences that change her as a person, to the extent that other people or the person herself may say that she is not the person she used to be (Paul 2014, 16–17; Ullmann-Margalit 2006, 158–59).[18] In my minimal, realistic model of the agent, if a choice giving rise to a personal transformative experience changes a person's core normative principles, then the person's self after that choice cannot be considered numerically identical to the self before the choice: they are two distinct agents.

Diachronic self-regarding decisions are also called diachronic *intrapersonal* decisions because they regard only the person facing the choice and her relationship with herself. I contend that, if we want to analyze the present-self–future-self relationship in diachronic self-regarding decisions, these decisions are better understood as *interagential*, in the sense of decisions between two agents. I support my interpretation of diachronic self-regarding decisions as interagential with two reasons. The first is that the present and future selves can be considered *as if* they were two distinct practical identities because the temporal stage at which a person's self is situated (i.e., this person's past, present, or future) determines some morally relevant characteristics of this self that are different from those of the person's selves situated at the other temporal stages, as I will show in section 4 (e.g., a person's present self has more decisional power than a person's future self). Considering the present and future selves as if they were distinct does not equate to contending that the two selves are metaphysically distinct entities, as the metaphysical level is not affected by a tendency of human moral psychology. Nor are the present and the future selves distinct entities at the practical level if they have the same core normative principles. The second reason supporting my interpretation of diachronic self-regarding decisions as interagential is the thesis that in diachronic self-regarding decisions that bring about personal transformative experiences involving a change of one's most important normative principles (i.e., the core ones), one's earlier and later selves are indeed numerically distinct agents. The latter statement regards the practical level of diachronic self-regarding decisions and thus does not entail the metaphysical thesis that the person before the personal transformative experiences is numerically different from the person after that experience.

3.4 The second step toward defending the morality of prudence: Justifying an action to oneself as a basic form of care for oneself

A practical agent is also a moral agent when she takes actions for which she can provide reasons that justify her actions to other agents. The definition of the moral agent as a subject who can justify her actions to others implies that her justification of actions has or tends to have an intersubjective validity that should be accepted by all, the agent herself included. This implication of the definition of the moral agent is the second step in defense of the thesis that prudence is moral. A basic form of an agent's care for another agent is the justification of her action to the latter. As a moral agent takes an action when this action is intersubjectively justified (therefore justified also to herself), the agent is in a moral relationship with herself and expresses a basic concern for herself. As Korsgaard puts it, "Acting is quite literally interacting with yourself" (2009, cit., 202).

Once taken the second step toward defending the morality of prudence, I can show the difference between my approach to the morality of prudence and that of Arvan (2020), who defends the same thesis, as seen in section 2.2. Arvan derives morality from prudence by contending that care for oneself includes care for others because the individual must include in her deliberation her possible future selves' interests in other human and nonhuman sentient beings. In other words, in his account, if the individual cares for her future self, she indirectly cares for other human and nonhuman sentient beings because she wants to avoid the possibility of causing her future self regret, which derives from the failure to care about those beings at an earlier time. In this derivation of morality from prudence, it seems that if the individual's present self does not care about, for instance, needy strangers, but must do that because the individual may develop an interest in needy strangers in the future, her present concern for needy strangers is not authentic but only derivative (i.e., it is derived from the possibility that a future self may be interested in needy strangers). Furthermore, if prudence is derived from morality, it seems that the value of other people is not a value per se (as they are morally equally worthy), but a value deriving from a sophisticated concern for oneself: the fact that one possible self of the individual may find other people valuable. In contrast, I defend the morality of prudence because I consider the latter a subset of morality. Prudence is the subset of morality in which the moral agent cares for herself; it is part of *self-regarding morality*, which regulates the individual's relationship with herself. In this section, I identified the first form of the moral agent's care for oneself: taking actions that can be justified to herself and other agents. In the next chapter,[19] I contend that caring for oneself means also protecting the very heart of morality: the moral agency of one's later selves.

4. The moral features of the present-self–future-self relationship and the interpretation of diachronic self-regarding decisions as cases of intergenerational ethics

In the previous section, I interpreted diachronic self-regarding decisions as interagential decisions. Next, I specify the kind of interagential relation that characterizes diachronic self-regarding decisions by examining the moral features of the present-self–future-self relationship. Three out of the four moral features are in common with those of the relation between contemporary people and future generations. These features indicate that the two relationships share a similar structure of decisional power, freedom, and knowledge. Therefore, I contend that the framework of interagential relationships that best describes diachronic self-regarding decisions is *intergenerational ethics*, namely, the branch of ethics regulating the relationship between present and future people. I consider diachronic self-regarding decisions as a special case of intergenerational ethics, in which the agents involved are one's present and later selves. Although Parfit (1984, 318) briefly mentioned that the agent's scarce care for her future self makes the latter similar to future generations, the interpretation of diachronic self-regarding decisions as a particular case of intergenerational ethics has not yet been proposed.

It may be objected that a fundamental difference between the present-self–future-self relationship and intergenerational relationships is the size of the temporal distance between the parties of the two relationships. In the present-self–future-self relationship, the maximal temporal distance is between the agent at the end of a person's life and the agent at the beginning of a person's life, whereas in intergenerational ethics, temporal distance can extend far in the future. I reply that the two temporal distances are a matter of order of magnitude that does not reduce the similarity in the structure (i.e., the moral features) of the two relationships.

The present self's diachronic self-regarding decisions affect the future self but the latter's decisions cannot affect the former.[20] Hence, one's earlier selves have more decisional power than one's later selves and may take advantage of their position in time. For example, the individual's present self may decide to favor her present desire to have a comfortable life and leave the future self with no savings for retirement. Given her greater decisional power, the present self can determine the end of the future self's existence or reduce its length; for instance, an earlier self could commit suicide or live a risky life that reduces the possibility that there will be a later self. This asymmetry is, however, not absolute. The future self has a veto power over the present self's plans and commitments: the future self can decide to abandon them. I call this power *self-regarding veto power*. Yet, the future self's self-regarding veto power is smaller than the present self's decisional power, as the former can only interrupt a project initiated by an earlier self, while the latter influences the later self's existence and identity. The *asymmetry of decisional power* is the first feature of the present-self–future-self relationship and shows a critical vulnerability of the future self. The asymmetry of decisional power is typical of intergenerational ethics:

52 Our relationship with our future selves

present people's decisions will affect future generations to the extent that present people's actions can determine whether there will be any future people at all (Jonas 1974, 1984). Moreover, future generations' actions do not affect the present generations, but they have a veto power with regard to projects and policies initiated by earlier generations.

Although the present self's decisions can strongly influence the future self's existence, the latter also depends on unpredictable events (e.g., an accident). Moreover, if the future self comes to exist, her identity—which is determined by her set of normative principles—is not already given, as it is partly influenced by the present self's decisions and partly by unpredictable life events. The *indeterminacy of the future self's identity and existence* is the second feature of the present-self–future-self relationship and parallels the indeterminacy of future generations' identities and existence.

In diachronic self-regarding decisions, the individual's present self does not know whether her future self will be happy with her choice or instead prefer that her earlier self had taken the other option. This is because the individual's present self does not know the future self's normative principles of action, existence, and events that will impact the future self. The present self can forecast and influence some of these elements, but she cannot know all the possible outcomes of her choices combined with how future events will affect the future self. As the present self's ignorance about the future self does not depend on the present self (i.e., she objectively cannot gain more information about the future), I call the present self's ignorance about the future self *objective ignorance*. This is the third feature of the present-self–future-self relationship. Objective ignorance also characterizes intergenerational relationships: present people do not know future generations' normative principles of actions, their needs, or what events will occur. This is one reason why some authors have contended that, in intergenerational ethics, it is difficult to precisely delineate present people's moral responsibility, if any, toward posterity (Callahan 1981, 78–80; Golding 1972, 97–98).

The fourth feature of the present-self–future-self relationship is the *strong causal relation* between these selves. This relation is stronger than that between two distinct persons (Shoemaker 1984, 89) and this strength is due to two factors, as explained in section 3.1. First, one's present and future selves are attributes or parts of the same person. Second, the mental states of a person's present self affect each subsequent mental state and thus decision, which have repercussions on this person's future self. The strong causal relation between one's present and future selves applies regardless of changes in the future self's core normative principles, as the individual's present self is the most capable of influencing her future self.[21] In intergenerational ethics, there is a direct causal relation between overlapping generations and an indirect causal relation between nonoverlapping generations. However, these relations lack the two factors founding the strong causal relation between one's present and future selves. Hence, I consider the strong causal connection between the present and future selves the only morally relevant characteristic that is not present in the relationship between contemporary people and future generations.

In conclusion, the moral features of the relationship between the present and future selves are (i) the decisional asymmetry between the two selves; (ii) the indeterminacy of the future self's identity and existence; (iii) the present self's objective ignorance of the future self's normative principles of action and existence, and events that will occur; and, finally, (iv) the strong causal relation between the two selves.

5. Conclusion

Diachronic self-regarding decisions involve an issue that most of modern and contemporary ethics has not considered as moral (i.e., prudence), and an issue that has been long debated in moral philosophy (i.e., the identity of the agent making such decisions). In this chapter, I discussed both topics and defended my position on them. I argued that prudence is a moral requirement because, first, imprudent acts cause harm to the future self that is not morally justified, and second, a basic form of one's care for oneself is the moral agent's justification of her actions to herself.

I then provided the minimal, realistic model of the agent, which is an empirically plausible account of the practical agent. The latter is the significant entity making diachronic self-regarding decisions, to whom I refer as a self. A self is an agent situated at a temporal stage of the person but not metaphysically distinct from the person. The minimal, realistic agent is a subject endowed with a set of normative principles of actions, a minimal temporal extension, and care for the future self that depends on the psychological connection with the latter. By applying my model of the agent to diachronic self-regarding decisions, I interpreted them as interagential decisions, namely, decisions between two agents: the present and future selves.

Lastly, I analyzed the morally relevant features of the relationship between the present and the future selves and found that that relationship shares three of four features with the moral relation between contemporary people and future generations: the asymmetry of decisional power, the indeterminacy of the identity and existence of the future self and future people, and the objective ignorance of the identity, existence, and conditions of the future self and future people. As these features of the present-self–future-self relationship determine a structure of decisional power, freedom, and knowledge similar to that of the present-people–future-generations relationship, I contended that the framework of interagential relationships that best describes diachronic self-regarding decisions is that of intergenerational ethics.

This chapter provided the theoretical basis for the Moral Theory of Prudence in diachronic self-regarding decisions that I develop in the next chapter. This theory consists of normative requirements that regulate what the present and future selves owe to each other in diachronic self-regarding decisions.

Notes

1. For an overview of the philosophical literature on well-being, see Crisp (2017).
2. Here, "value" is broadly conceived of as something of worth to the individual that gives her a reason to act.
3. For the relationship between prudence and morality, see Kaspar (2011); Fremstedal (2018); Tiberius (2002), (2008, ch. 7); Berman (2014); Schmidtz (1997); Scanlon (1998, 136–43).
4. See Bratman (2012, 2018); Hedden (2015a, 2015b); Hubin (1980); Dorsey (2021).
5. See Nagel (1970, part II); Huckfeldt (2011); Bratman (2018, ch. 10); Das (2003).
6. This, however, does not mean that Kant overlooks the individual's relationship with herself, as Kant addresses the duties to oneself. Yet duties to oneself have nothing to do with prudence in Kant's moral system: they are impersonal and impartial rules of actions that pertain to the respect for one's own humanity or being worthy of this humanity (Kant 1991 [1797], 6:417–47: 214–42); thus, they are detached from the pursuit of happiness.
7. In modern ethics, Hume also considers prudence as a moral virtue. However, although he considers prudence a natural ability that can be considered moral, he does not deal with it at length—rather, he only mentions such a characterization (Hume 1928 [1738–1740], III.iii.3: 606–11).
8. Parfit's approach to metaphysical identity aims to demonstrate that what matters in assessing whether two subjects are the same person is the chain of interrelated psychological states among them, not their identity relation (Parfit 1984, 210–11; Shoemaker 2019).
9. The agent-relative part of a moral theory concerns the agent's special obligations to persons with whom she has special relations.
10. I think that, in Parfit's framework, the strategy of including prudence in the agent-relative part of a moral theory is more promising than conceiving prudence as an agent-neutral principle of beneficence. Considering the requirements of prudence as impersonal duties deriving from beneficence considerably reduces their normative force. In fact, impersonal duties are overridden by more stringent duties such as one's agent-relative obligations toward some closely related persons or the general claim of others not to be maltreated in certain ways. This leads to the consequence that an individual can take care of her future self only when duties towards others are fulfilled. However, if one does not take care of her future self or does so only after duties to others are fulfilled,

it is likely that at some point in the future, one will be unable to fulfill one's duties toward others because, as one's earlier self neglected one's later self, the latter is incapable of taking care of others. It is reasonable to expect that one's care for oneself is something more than an impersonal duty in light of the fact that, in Parfit's framework, the present and the future selves are in a special relationship, as they are connected through relation R.

11. See Chapter 3, section 4.
12. See, for instance, Nagel (1970); Rawls (1999); Brink (2003, 2011); Korsgaard (2009).
13. See section 2.2.
14. See Chapter 3, section 2.4.
15. For simplicity, I assume here the biological account of personal identity (i.e., sameness of body) (DeGrazia 2005; Olson 1997). However, my account does not hinge on this assumption, as I disregard the relevance of metaphysical identity in the moral evaluation of diachronic self-regarding decisions, as I explain later in this section.
16. Korsgaard (2009, 58) admits that she did not find a principle of prudence with such characteristics and called it the "missing principle."
17. See section 2.3.
18. Paul distinguishes two kinds of transformative experiences: personal transformative experiences (those that transform who an individual is) and epistemic transformative experiences (those that transform what an individual knows and provide her with new experiences) (Paul 2014, 16–17, Paul 2020, 17). Usually personal transformative experiences are radically new experiences and thus they are also epistemic transformative experiences (Paul 2014, 16–17, 2020, 17).
19. See Chapter 3, section 2.4.
20. The individual's later self can reinterpret the earlier self's actions by giving them a different meaning, but she cannot change what the earlier self did.
21. I do not consider the case of a person's self (A's self) being completely manipulated by another person's self (B's self) because, in such cases, A's self cannot be considered an agent, namely a subject that autonomously takes actions.

References

Annas, Julia. 1995. "Prudence and Morality in Ancient and Modern Ethics." *Ethics* 105: 241–57.
Anscombe, G. E. M. 1957. *Intention*. Oxford: Basil Blackwell.
Aristotle. 2000. *Nichomachean Ethics*. Edited by R. Crisp. Cambridge: Cambridge University Press. https://doi.org/10.7208/chicago/9780226026763.001.0001.
Arvan, Marcus. 2020. *Neurofunctional Prudence and Morality*. New York: Routledge.
Bartels, Daniel M., and Oleg Urminsky. 2011. "On Intertemporal Selfishness: How the Perceived Instability of Identity Underlies Impatient Consumption." *Journal of Consumer Research* 38 (1): 182–98. https://doi.org/10.1086/658339.
———. 2015. "To Know and to Care: How Awareness and Valuation of the Future Jointly Shape Consumer Spending." *Journal of Consumer Research* 41 (6): 1469–85. https://doi.org/10.1086/680670.n.

Berman, Scott. 2014. "Prudence and Morality: Socrates Versus Moral Philosophers." *South African Journal of Philosophy* 33 (4): 381–94. https://doi.org/10.1 080/02580136.2014.967591.

Bratman, Michael E. 2012. "Time, Rationality, and Self-Governance." *Philosophical Issues* 22: 73–88.

———. 2018. *Planning, Time, and Self-Governance: Essays in Practical Rationality*. Oxford University Press. https://doi.org/10.1093/oso/9780190867850.001.0001.

Brink, David O. 2003. "Prudence and Authenticity: Intrapersonal Conflicts of Value." *Philosophical Review* 112 (2): 215–45. https://doi.org/10.1215/00318108-112-2-215.

———. 2011. "Prospects for Temporal Neutrality." In *The Oxford Handbook of Philosophy of Time*, edited by C. Callender. Oxford: Oxford University Press. https://doi.org/10.1093/oxfordhb/9780199298204.003.0012.

Bruckner, Donald W. 2003. "A Contractarian Account of (Part of) Prudence." *American Philosophical Quarterly* 40 (1): 33–46. https://doi.org/10.2307/20010095.

Callahan, Daniel. 1981. "What Obligations Do We Have to Future Generations?" In *Responsibilities to Future Generations*, edited by E. Partridge. New York: Prometeus.

Chapman, Gretchen B. 1996. "Temporal Discounting and Utility for Health and Money." *Journal of Experimental Psychology. Learning, Memory, and Cognition* 22 (3): 771–91. https://doi.org/10.1037/0278-7393.22.3.771.

Chapman, Gretchen B., and A. S. Elstein. 1995. "Valuing the Future: Temporal Discounting of Health and Money." *Medical Decision Making: An International Journal of the Society for Medical Decision Making* 15 (4): 373–86. https://doi.org/10.1177/0272989X9501500408.

Crisp, Roger. 2017. "Well-Being." In *Stanford Encyclopedia of Philosophy*, edited by E. N. Zalta. Accessed July 31, 2021. https://plato.stanford.edu/archives/fall2017/entries/well-being/.

Cureton, Adam. 2016. "Prudence and Responsibility to Self in an Identity Crisis." *Res Philosophica* 93 (4): 815–41. https://doi.org/10.11612/resphil.1466.

Das, Ramon. 2003. "Prudence, Identity, and Value." In *Time and Ethics: Essays at the Intersection*, edited by H. L. Dyke. Dordrecht: Springer. https://doi.org/10.1007/978-94-017-3530-8_3.

Davidson, Donald. 1963. "Actions, Reasons, and Causes." *The Journal of Philosophy* 60 (23): 685–700. https://doi.org/10.2307/2023177.

DeGrazia, David. 2005. *Human Identity and Bioethics*. Cambridge: Cambridge University Press.

Den Uyl, Douglas J. 1991. *The Virtue of Prudence*. New York: Peter Lang.

Dorsey, Dale. 2021. *A Theory of Prudence*. Oxford: Oxford University Press. https://doi.org/10.1093/oso/9780198823759.001.0001.

Ersner-Hershfield, Hal, G. Elliott Wimmer, and Brian Knutson. 2009. "Saving for the Future Self: Neural Measures of Future Self-Continuity Predict Temporal Discounting." *Social Cognitive and Affective Neuroscience* 4 (1): 85–92. https://doi.org/10.1093/scan/nsn042.

Frankfurt, Harry G. 1971. "Freedom of the Will and the Concept of a Person." *The Journal of Philosophy* 68 (1): 5–20. https://doi.org/10.2307/2024717.

Fremstedal, Roe. 2018. "Morality and Prudence: A Case for Substantial Overlap and Limited Conflict." *Journal of Value Inquiry* 52 (1): 1–16. https://doi.org/10.1007/s10790-017-9598-5.

Golding, Martin P. 1972. "Obligations to Future Generations." *Monist* 56 (1): 85–99. https://doi.org/10.5840/monist197256118.

Hausman, Jerry A. 1979. "Individual Discount Rates and the Purchase and Utilization of Energy-Using Durables." *The Bell Journal of Economics* 10 (1): 33–54. https://doi.org/10.2307/3003318.

Hedden, Brian. 2015a. *Reasons Without Persons: Rationality, Identity, and Time*. New York: Oxford University Press.

———. 2015b. "Time-Slice Rationality." *Mind* 124 (494): 449–91. https://doi.org/10.1093/mind/fzu181.

Hershfield, Hal E., Daniel G. Goldstein, William F. Sharpe, Jesse Fox, Leo Yeykelis, Laura L. Carstensen, and Jeremy N. Bailenson. 2011. "Increasing Saving Behavior Through Age-Progressed Renderings of the Future Self." *Journal of Marketing Research* 48: S23–S37. https://doi.org/10.1509/jmkr.48.SPL.S23.

Hubin, Clayton D. 1980. "Prudential Reasons." *Canadian Journal of Philosophy* 10 (1): 63–81. https://doi.org/10.1080/00455091.1980.10716283.

Huckfeldt, Vaughn. 2011. "Prudence, Commitments and Intertemporal Conflicts." *Theoria* 77 (1): 42–54. https://doi.org/10.1111/j.1755-2567.2010.01084.x.

Hume, David. 1928 [1738–1740]. *A Treatise of Human Nature*. Edited by L. A. Selby-Bigge. Oxford: Clarendon Press.

Irwin, Terence H. 1995. "Prudence and Morality in Greek Ethics." *Ethics* 105 (2): 284–95. http://www.jstor.org/stable/2382346.

Jonas, Hans. 1974. "Technology and Responsibility: The Ethics of an Endangered Future." In *Responsibilities to Future Generations*, edited by E. Partridge. 1981. New York: Prometeus.

———. 1984. *The Imperative of Responsibility: In Search of an Ethics for the Technological Age*. Chicago and London: University of Chicago Press.

Kant, Immanuel. 1991 [1797]. *The Metaphysics of Morals*. Edited by M. J. Gregor. Cambridge: Cambridge University Press. https://doi.org/10.1017/9781316091388.

———. 2006 [1785]. *Groundwork of the Metaphysics of Morals*. Edited by M. J. Gregor. Cambridge: Cambridge University Press.

Kaspar, David. 2011. "Can Morality Do Without Prudence?" *Philosophia* 39: 311–26.

Korsgaard, Christine M. 1989. "Personal Identity and the Unity of Agency: A Kantian Response to Parfit." *Philosophy & Public Affairs* 18 (2): 101–32.

———. 1996. *The Sources of Normativity*. New York: Cambridge University Press.

———. 2009. *Self-Constitution: Agency, Identity, and Integrity. Self-Constitution: Agency, Identity, and Integrity*. Oxford: Oxford University Press. https://doi.org/10.1093/acprof:oso/9780199552795.001.0001.

McKerlie, Dennis. 2007. "Rational Choice, Changes in Values Over Time, and Well-Being." *Utilitas* 19 (1): 51–72. https://doi.org/10.1017/S0953820806002342.

Mele, Alfred R. 2003. *Motivation and Agency*. New York: Oxford University Press. https://doi.org/10.1093/019515617X.001.0001.

Mill, John Stuart. 2003 [1859]. "On Liberty." In *Utilitarianism and On Liberty*, edited by M. Warnock. Malden, MA: Blackwell Publishing.

Mitchell, Jason P., Jessica Schirmer, Daniel L. Ames, and Daniel T. Gilbert. 2011. "Medial Prefrontal Cortex Predicts Intertemporal Choice." *Journal of Cognitive Neuroscience* 23 (4): 857–66. https://doi.org/10.1162/jocn.2010.21479.

Morton, Jennifer M. 2013. "Deliberating for Our Far Future Selves." *Ethical Theory and Moral Practice*. https://doi.org/10.1007/s10677-012-9391-2.

Nagel, Thomas. 1970. *The Possibility of Altruism*. Oxford: Oxford University Press.

Neblett, William. 1969. "Morality, Prudence, and Obligations to Oneself." *Ethics* 80 (1): 70–73. https://doi.org/10.1086/291752.

Nussbaum, Shiri, Yaacov Trope, and Nira Liberman. 2003. "Creeping Dispositionism: The Temporal Dynamics of Behavior Prediction." *Journal of Personality and Social Psychology* 84 (3): 485–97. https://doi.org/10.1037/0022-3514.84.3.485.

Olson, Eric T. 1997. *The Human Animal: Personal Identity Without Psychology*. New York: Oxford University Press.

Parfit, Derek. 1971. "Personal Identity." *The Philosophical Review* 80 (1): 3–27. https://doi.org/10.1007/s11017-010-9147-8.

———. 1984. *Reasons and Persons*. Oxford: Clarendon Press.

Paul, Laurie Ann. 2014. *Transformative Experience*. Oxford: Oxford University Press. https://doi.org/10.1093/acprof:oso/9780198717959.001.0001.

———. 2020. "Who Will I Become?" In *Becoming Someone New: Essays on Transformative Experience, Choice, and Change*, edited by E. Lambert and J. Schwenkler. Oxford: Oxford University Press.

Pettigrew, Richard. 2020. *Choosing for Changing Selves*. Oxford: Oxford University Press.

Pronin, Emily, Christopher Y. Olivola, and Kathleen A. Kennedy. 2008. "Doing Unto Future Selves As You Would Do Unto Others: Psychological Distance and Decision Making." *Personality and Social Psychology Bulletin* 34 (2): 224–36. https://doi.org/10.1177/0146167207310023.

Pronin, Emily, and Lee Ross. 2006. "Temporal Differences in Trait Self-Ascription: When the Self Is Seen as an Other." *Journal of Personality and Social Psychology* 90 (2): 197–209. https://doi.org/10.1037/0022-3514.90.2.197.

Rasmussen, Erin B., Steven R. Lawyer, and William Reilly. 2010. "Percent Body Fat Is Related to Delay and Probability Discounting for Food in Humans." *Behavioural Processes* 83 (1): 23–30. https://doi.org/10.1016/j.beproc.2009.09.001.

Rawls, John. 1999. *A Theory of Justice: Revised Edition*. Cambridge: Belknap Press. https://doi.org/10.1080/713659260.

Scanlon, Thomas. 1998. *What We Owe to Each Other*. Cambridge: Belknap Press.

Schmidtz, David. 1997. "Self-interest: What's in it for Me?" *Social Philosophy and Policy* 14 (1): 107–21. https://doi.org/10.1017/s0265052500001692.

Shoemaker, David. 2019. "Personal Identity and Ethics." In *Stanford Encyclopedia of Philosophy*, edited by E. N. Zalta. Accessed July 31, 2021. https://plato.stanford.edu/archives/win2019/entries/identity-ethics/.

Shoemaker, Sidney. 1984. "Personal Identity: A Materialist's Account." In *Personal Identity*, edited by S. Shoemaker and R. Swinburne. Oxford: Blackwell.

Sidgwick, Henry. 1962 [1874]. *The Methods of Ethics*. London and Toronto: Palgrave Macmillan.

Smith, Adam. 1976 [1790]. "The Theory of Moral Sentiments." In *The Glasgow Edition of the Works and Correspondence of Adam Smith*, edited by D. D. Raphael and A. L. Macfie, Vol. I. Oxford: Clarendon Press.

Strawson, Galen. 2004. "Against Narrativity." *Ratio* 17 (4): 428–52. https://doi.org/10.1111/j.1467-9329.2004.00264.x.

Tiberius, Valerie. 2002. "Perspective: A Prudential Virtue." *American Philosophical Quarterly*. https://doi.org/10.2307/20010082.

———. 2008. *The Reflective Life: Living Wisely With Our Limits*. New York: Oxford University Press. https://doi.org/10.1111/j.1467-9213.2009.639_4.x.

Timmermann, Jens. 2006. "Kantian Duties to the Self, Explained and Defended." *Philosophy* 81 (317): 505–30.

Ullmann-Margalit, Edna. 2006. "Big Decisions: Opting, Converting, Drifting." *Royal Institute of Philosophy Supplement* 58: 157–72.

Viganò, Eleonora. 2017. "Not Just an Inferior Virtue, nor Self-Interest: Adam Smith on Prudence." *Journal of Scottish Philosophy* 15 (1): 125–43. https://doi.org/10.3366/jsp.2017.0155.

3 How should we treat our future selves? The moral requirements of prudence to one's present and future selves

1. Introduction

In the second chapter, I elaborated the theoretical basis of my normative theory guiding one's present self in diachronic self-regarding decisions, which involve oneself and have consequences for one's future self. The first element of the theoretical basis of my approach is the thesis that prudence as care for oneself is moral, which is based on two arguments: first, imprudent acts harm one's future self; and second, a moral agent exhibits basic care for herself when she justifies her actions to the other agents and thus also to herself. The second element of the theoretical basis of my approach to diachronic self-regarding decisions is an empirically plausible model of the human agent (i.e., the minimal, realistic model of the agent), to whom I refer as self. A person's self is an agent that is situated at a temporal stage of the person and coexists with the person. The agent of the minimal, realistic model is minimally temporally extended and is characterized by a set of normative principles of action and care for the future self, which depends on her perceived psychological connection with the future self. The third element of the theoretical basis of my approach is the set of morally relevant features of the present-self–future-self relationship: the asymmetry of decisional power between the two selves; the indeterminacy of the future self's identity and existence; the present self's objective ignorance of the future self's identity and existence, and future events that will occur; and the strong causal relation between the two selves.

The aim of this chapter is to defend a normative theory of prudence regulating the relationship between one's present and future selves and guiding one's present self in diachronic self-regarding decisions: the *Moral Theory of Prudence in diachronic self-regarding decisions*. First, I elaborate the normative requirements of diachronic self-regarding decisions, which constitute the Moral Theory of Prudence in diachronic self-regarding decisions.

DOI: 10.4324/9781003122142-4

This theory consists of three principles: (i) the *obligation to preserve one's future agency*, (ii) the *right to an open present*, and (iii) *forward-looking self-regarding responsibility*. The obligation to preserve one's future agency requires one's present self to avoid choices that jeopardize the necessary conditions for the pursuit of any set of normative principles of action. The future self's right to an open present consists of the future self's claim to pursue her set of normative principles of action. Forward-looking self-regarding responsibility refers to the present self's responsibility to the future self for the predictable effects of the present self's actions on the future self. I also contend that, in my Moral Theory of Prudence, prudence is a moral requirement because prudence as care for oneself applied to the relationship between one's earlier and later selves requires protecting the very heart of morality: moral agency.

I then discuss the possible objections that may be raised against my approach to diachronic self-regarding decisions. Some derive from the typical problems that every normative account regarding one's future selves encounters, namely, the impossibility of attributing moral claims to a not-yet-existent agent (i.e., the future self), the intrapersonal nonidentity problem arising from the future self's indeterminacy, and the possibility that one's future self will never come to exist. Other objections are specific to the moral requirements of my theory: the impossibility of having obligations to oneself, the absence of backward-looking self-regarding responsibility in the case of identity change, and the irrelevance of establishing forward-looking self-regarding responsibility.

Finally, I discuss the current philosophical positions on diachronic self-regarding decisions and identify the differences between them and the Moral Theory of Prudence.

2. The Moral Theory of Prudence in diachronic self-regarding decisions

The Moral Theory of Prudence in diachronic self-regarding decisions regulates the relationship between a person's present and future selves. Its requirements descend from the features of the present-self–future-self relationship and the minimal, realistic account of practical identity. In other words, the features of their relationship and their characterization as minimal, realistic agents make it fitting (i.e., appropriate) to derive such requirements. The latter are pro tanto moral requirements, namely, they provide a reason to act on their basis, but they can be trumped by other moral considerations. As the present-self–future-self relationship involves prudence (i.e., care for oneself) and I consider prudence a moral requirement, I define this theory of prudence as moral.

In this section, I present the normative requirements of my theory and take the last step to support the thesis that prudence is moral by showing that the requirements of my theory protect the condition of being a moral agent. In the next section, I respond to the main possible objections to my theory.

2.1 The present self's obligation to preserve the future self's agency

Although the present self's decisions influence the future self's existence and identity (i.e., her set of normative principles), the future self is not completely defined at the time that a diachronic self-regarding decision is made. The future self is not present at the time of the decision: she is yet to come. This is the cause of the future self's vulnerability and the present self's objective ignorance about the future self's normative principles and existence. The indeterminacy of the future self in the present-self–future-self relationship is the main difference between this relationship and the usual moral relationships we have with contemporary parties. This indeterminacy makes it difficult to regulate the relationship between one's present and future selves. In fact, it gives rise to the problem of multiple future selves: in diachronic self-regarding decisions, there can be infinite possibly occurring future selves of a person, depending on the present self's choices and future events that will occur. However, as long as the future self is an agent,[1] the essential components of her agency (i.e., her being an agent) are known. The present self knows that the future self will have a set of normative principles motivating her actions. The latter component of agency enables one to determine the first two moral requirements of the present-self–future-self relationship without the need to specify how one's future self will be and which normative principles she will pursue, thus solving the problem of multiple future selves.

Given the asymmetry of decisional power, the present self may prevent the future self from the pursuit of the future self's set of normative principles; for instance, the present self could decrease the future self's lifespan through unhealthy choices. This action is not morally justified because it is based on an asymmetrical relation of decisional power that results only from the direction of time and causality. The future and present selves have the same characteristics as agents and thus are equally entitled to pursue their own normative principles.[2]

As I argue in more detail when discussing objections to my theory,[3] I contend that the equal moral worth of a person's diachronic selves is not undermined by the temporal position of such selves in a person's life. In other words, the *not-yet-existence* of one's future self does not make a difference in the moral worth of this self as an agent; thus, rights can be attributed to the future self. The first requirement of the Moral Theory of Prudence is grounded in three statements: (a) the present and future selves are both agents and thus equally entitled to pursue their own normative principles; (b) a self's temporal location in a person's life does not affect that self's moral worth and thus agency; and (c) in terms of decisional power, a person's present self is more free than her future self solely because the former precedes the latter. I derive two considerations from these statements. First, a person's present self is not justified in undertaking actions that prevent this person's future self from pursuing her set of normative principles. Second, the present self should not hinder the future self's pursuit of the future self's normative principles and the future self should not hinder the present self's pursuit of the present self's normative principles. On the basis of these two considerations, the Moral Theory of Prudence in diachronic self-regarding decisions requires a diachronic self-regarding obligation of the present self: preserving the future self's agency so that the future self can pursue her normative principles, compatibly with the present self's possibility of pursuing her own ones. This obligation ensures the future self the same conditions of action of the present self: both should be able to pursue their own sets of normative principles.

The future self's set of normative principles is not known yet in the present, but this does not mean that the present self should avoid making choices that jeopardize the pursuit of any set of normative principles. This request would be too demanding and hinder the present self's pursuit of her own set of normative principles. The obligation to preserve the future self's agency descends from the features of the present-self–future-self relationship and the minimal, realistic account of practical identity so it has to be based on them. In particular, the equal claim of the present and future selves to pursue their own sets and the objective ignorance of the future self's set specify the requirement of such an obligation: the present self should make choices that, while enabling the pursuit of her set, enable the future self to change the life path taken by the present self, in case the future self will have a different set. As a consequence, the obligation to preserve the future self's agency requires to make choices that do not jeopardize the necessary conditions for the pursuit of any set of normative principles.

The necessary conditions for the pursuit of any set of normative principles are the elements that enable the pursuit of each possible set of normative principles that a person's self can choose. Specifying the exact index of such conditions is out of the scope and aim of the Moral Theory of Prudence, as the latter is not a theory of the good life. Yet I can list some necessary conditions on which we expect an overlapping consensus among various approaches to agency and the good life, such as health, adequate education, income, and basic rights like the freedom to develop and express critical thought. Nussbaum's ten central *capabilities* could be read as necessary conditions for the pursuit of any set of normative principles (Nussbaum 2006, 76–78). The capabilities are the set of means that enable people to achieve the doing and beings that they want to achieve (Sen 1979, 1999, 2009; Nussbaum 2000, 2006). Rawls' primary goods could be considered as necessary conditions for the pursuit of any set as well. In Rawls' theory of justice, primary goods enable citizens of a well-ordered society to pursue a wide range of rational plans of life. There are natural primary goods such as health and vigor and social primary goods such as basic rights and liberties, income and wealth, and self-respect (Rawls 1999, 79, 380, 386, 2001, 57–59). Of course, if a necessary condition is partly independent of a person's actions such as health, the present self is required to protect the aspects of such a condition on which she has control; for instance, she should not smoke.

Let us see what the obligation to preserve the future self's agency requires in practice in the diachronic self-regarding decision of whether to dedicate oneself to an athletic career early in life. When making such a choice, one does not know whether one's future self will approve of the earlier self's professional training and sacrifice of opportunities of education in favor of the athletic career. The Moral Theory of Prudence requires a young athlete who wants to become a professional athlete to make choices granting her a complementary education and at the same time her current specialization in the athletic career. A complementary education is a necessary condition for the pursuit of any set of normative principles—as it lays the basis for the pursuit of different careers in the future—while the specialization in the athletic career is part of the young athlete's current set of normative principles.

It is noteworthy that the present self's obligation to preserve the future self's agency does not imply value judgments of a self's set of normative principles. The aim of the Moral Theory of Prudence is not to guide the agent to find the best or most valuable set of normative principles; rather, it is to guide a person's present self in making a diachronic self-regarding decision that preserves the agency of this person's future self, namely, one that enables the future self to pursue her normative principles.

It may seem that the obligation to preserve the future self's agency is incompatible with the very process of making a decision, which necessarily requires the selection of an option and the exclusion of the alternatives. Such a process may be interpreted as violating the present self's obligation to preserve the future self's agency. However, the obligation to preserve the future self's agency does not mean always keeping a self's options open and ready to be chosen. Rather, it involves choosing options that, by protecting the necessary conditions for the pursuit of any set of normative principles, enable one's future self to take a different life path in case the path on which she finds herself (i.e., the path "inherited" from the earlier self) is not consistent with her set of normative principles. For the same reason, the obligation to preserve the future self's agency does not conflict with one's long-term life plan. In fact, one's present self is free to pursue a long-term plan as long as she does not undermine the necessary conditions that enable one's future self to pursue her set of normative principles.

2.2 The future self's right to an open present

The present self's obligation to preserve the future self's agency can be postulated as the counterpart of the right to an open present that I attribute to the future self. The right to an open present is the application to the future self of the *right to an open future* that Feinberg (1992) attributes to children. Feinberg's right to an open future arises from a case of intergenerational ethics regarding overlapping generations, namely parents and children. It consists of autonomy rights that are to be preserved for the child until she is an adult and that can be violated in advance by the parents. This violation consists of cutting off certain key options in the present that the child will no longer have when she will be adult.

Since my approach involves practical agents, I propose attributing the right to an open future to one's future self. The latter will exist in the future, but at the time in which she exists, her agency is present, not future. Therefore, I call this right the future self's right to an open present. The right to an open present consists of the future self's claim to pursue her set of normative principles of action. As seen, each diachronic self of a person is entitled to pursue her own set of normative principles. Therefore, the future self's right to an open present is limited, like the obligation to preserve the future self's agency, by the present self's right to pursue her set of normative principles. The reciprocal limitation that each self of a person exercises on the other ones in my Moral Theory of Prudence is a form of fairness to oneself (Arvan 2020, 64, 79): each self has the same right to an open present toward the earlier selves and owes the same obligation to preserve the future agency to the later selves.[4] This reciprocal limitation avoids that a person's self is favored over the other diachronic selves of a person or sacrifices more than them.

Feinberg contends that the adult's right to autonomy prevents the right to an open future from being ascribed to the individual's future self, for the adult's present autonomy "takes precedence even over his probable future good" (Feinberg 1992, cit., 78). In contrast, I attribute this right to the future self for two reasons. First, in the minimal, realistic model of practical identity, I consider one's diachronic selves as if they were numerically distinct and contend that they are actually distinct if one changes her core normative principles. Second, the child's and future self's moral positions are similar in that neither can defend her own present interests against the other party in the relationship (i.e., the parents or present self, respectively). Moreover, the existence, identity, and future conditions of both the child and future self are highly affected by the other party and not completely known in the present. I hold that the future self's right to an open present does not conflict with the present self's autonomy because in the Moral Theory of Prudence, this right does not prevent the present self from pursuing her set of normative principles.

I define the principle to protect the future self's open present as a right because, first, it is an application of Feinberg's right to an open future and, second, the language of rights gives precise expression to a structure of decisional power and freedom, such as that of diachronic self-regarding decisions. The individual's present self has more decisional power than the individual's future self; with this power, the present self can limit the future self's justified freedom to pursue her set of normative principles (justified because the future self is an agent). However, I subscribe neither to a theory of rights nor to a rights-based morality.[5]

The right to an open present provides an argument in favor of the pro tanto moral impermissibility of suicide. Suicide can partly be considered a diachronic self-regarding decision because it significatively involves oneself and has consequences for one's later self. It is only partly a diachronic self-regarding decision because it also involves other people, for instance, the relatives and friends of the person committing suicide. Suicide is an interrupted diachronic self-regarding decision because, in such a choice, we cannot say that the future self is not yet existent; rather, the future self will not exist. Committing suicide closes the future self's present by nullifying her possibility to pursue her set of normative principles. Therefore, suicide violates the future self's right to an open present. This right supports only pro tanto—and not absolutely—the moral wrongness of suicide for two reasons. First, suicide is a diachronic self-regarding decision only in part. Thus, other moral requirements descending from one's relationships with other people may override that right. Second, the Moral Theory of Prudence regulates one aspect of one's life (i.e., the moral relation between one's present and future selves in diachronic self-regarding decisions) through pro tanto principles. Thus, the theory admits that other self-regarding moral principles are involved in a high-stakes decision such as suicide and can be weightier than the right to an open present. For instance, the present self's requirement to cease the pain due to a terminal illness or a condition of constant suffering may override the future self's right to an open present.

In the previous chapter,[6] I showed that the future self has self-regarding veto power over the present self's plans and commitments, in the sense that the future self can abandon them. The right to an open present justifies the future self's use of self-regarding veto power in case the latter is different from the earlier self (i.e., the future self has a different set of core normative principles). In fact, if the present and future selves are different, the future self will limit her life options and plans if she pursues the earlier self's plans. The future self's adherence to a decision made by the earlier self that the former neither shares nor supports is a lack of authenticity,[7] as in this case the future self's behavior is not befitting of a practical agent, who pursues her set of normative principles and not the set of another agent (i.e., the earlier self). Conversely, if the future self is identical to the present self, the two have the same core normative principles, and it would make no sense for the future self to stop pursuing plans that she herself wants to carry out.

My justification of the case in which the future self should exercise self-regarding veto power is similar to the conclusion that Bykvist (2003) reached, in his *harmony view*, regarding conflicts of preferences between an individual's past and present selves. Such preferences can be considered as a component of an agent's set of normative principles. For Bykvist, when making a choice, the present self should take into account the past self's preference that a state of affairs take place at a later time (thus in the present self's time) only if the past self's preference is sustained by the present self's preferences (Bykvist 2003, 124). In other words, one's past preferences count only if they are the same as one's present preferences.

2.3 The present self's forward-looking self-regarding responsibility

The last principle of the Moral Theory of Prudence regards the present self's moral responsibility, namely responsibility based on moral considerations (Talbert 2019; van de Poel 2011, 37). Two kinds of responsibilities are relevant in a theory regulating the present-self–future-self relationship: *forward-looking* and *backward-looking* responsibilities.

In my framework reading diachronic self-regarding decisions as interagential, I conceive of forward-looking responsibility as the relation in which one's self is responsible in the present to one's later self for an action that the present self takes and its consequences in the future. Notwithstanding the longstanding debate on moral responsibility and its attribution, many philosophical approaches agree on at least three conditions for the attribution of forward-looking responsibility (e.g., Jonas 1984, 90; Noorman 2020): (i) there is a causal connection between the agent and the outcome of her actions—that is, she has causal influence and control over the occurrence of the outcome; (ii) the agent is able to consider the possible consequences of her actions; and (iii) she chooses freely, namely without being forced by other individuals. In the relationship between the present and future selves, I verify whether the three conditions for the attribution of forward-looking responsibility are fulfilled in diachronic self-regarding decisions. The choice made by the present self in a diachronic self-regarding decision is controlled by her—that is, the present self could have decided differently— and, in light of the strong causal relation between the present and future selves and the direction of causality and time, her decision affects the future self. Therefore, condition (i) is fulfilled. The strong causal relation is the fourth feature of the present-self–future-self relationship that I described in Chapter 2. The present self is aware of the effects of her action on the future self that are predictable at the moment of the decision, thus condition (ii) is fulfilled. The present self is not responsible, however, for consequences that she cannot foresee because of objective ignorance (the third feature of the present-self–future-self relationship). Condition (iii) is assumed by default because diachronic self-regarding decisions concern the individual's relationship with herself. If another individual forces or influences the agent's choice in a diachronic self-regarding decision, the decision is no longer self-regarding. The three conditions for ascribing forward-looking responsibility to the present self with regard to her decisions affecting the future self are thus satisfied in diachronic self-regarding decisions. As responsibility usually regards interpersonal relationships, I call the present self's responsibility to the future self *forward-looking self-regarding responsibility*.

In my framework, in which diachronic self-regarding decisions are interagential, I conceive of *backward-looking self-regarding responsibility* as the relation in which one's self is responsible in the present for a past action taken by one's earlier self. Is such a responsibility applicable to the future self for the actions undertaken by the present self? This question cannot be answered within the framework of the Moral Theory of Prudence because doing so requires taking a stance on the relationship between backward-looking responsibility and personal identity— and thus a position in the metaphysical debate on personal identity. In fact, answering this question would require me to defend a substantial theory on backward-looking responsibility—namely, to establish whether this responsibility depends on the relation of identity between selves, on Parfit's relation R, or on another relation among one's successive selves.[8] This cannot be settled through the framework of the Moral Theory of Prudence, which comprises the four features of the present-self–future-self relationship and the account of the practical agent. Therefore, with regard to responsibility in diachronic self-regarding decisions, the Moral Theory of Prudence establishes only forward-looking self-regarding responsibility.

2.4 The third step toward defending the morality of prudence: The protection of moral agency in the Moral Theory of Prudence

In the previous chapter, I took the first two steps toward defending the morality of prudence. I contended that, first, prudence is a moral requirement because it avoids some conduct that harm the individual's future self;[9] and, second, moral agents have a basic care for themselves, which consists of justifying their actions to themselves.[10] Now, I take the final step in defense of the morality of prudence.

My normative theory of diachronic self-regarding decisions is based on an account of practical identity that admits the possibility that an agent does not temporally extend to the duration of a person's life. Within a framework of practical identity that admits this possibility, the future self's agency—which includes moral agency (i.e., taking actions whose reasons are intersubjectively justifiable)—can be threatened by the present self's choices. The future self is an agent, and being an agent entails pursuing one's set of normative principles. As the present self's advantageous position in time can limit the future self's agency, the Moral Theory of Prudence requires the present self to preserve the future self's agency and grants the future self the right to an open present. In my theory, prudence as care for oneself is moral because that care is regulated by two moral requirements (namely, the obligation to preserve the future self's agency and the right to an open present) that protect a fundamental component of agency: pursuing one's set of normative principles. Agency is at the heart of morality, as being an agent is a necessary condition for being moral, that is, for moral agency. In other words, in the Moral Theory of Prudence, if the individual's present self respects the normative requirements of the theory, she is prudent in the sense that she cares for the future self by protecting the latter's agency.

3. Replies to the main objections to the Moral Theory of Prudence

In this section, I address the main objections that may be raised against my Moral Theory of Prudence in diachronic self-regarding decisions.

3.1 The attribution of a right to a not yet (and maybe never) existing self

As anticipated, my Moral Theory of Prudence is not a theory of rights, although one of its normative requirements is the future self's right to an open present. I am open to the possibility that the principle of protecting the future self's open present cannot be defined as a right under some theories of rights, such as the will theory.[11] However, I maintain that this principle has a normative force, even if it is not a right according to some theories. It can be more generally interpreted as the future self's moral claim that arises from the present-self–future-self relationship and her being an agent and that results in a moral obligation of the present self—specifically, the obligation to preserve the future self's agency.

One main objection may be raised against the attribution of a right or moral claim to one's future self. In intergenerational ethics, the view according to which rights are predicted of existing beings rejects the attribution of rights to future generations (Beckerman and Pasek 2001, 15; De George 1981; Macklin 1981). Similarly, in this view, it may be objected that the future self does not exist at the time of a diachronic self-regarding decision and thus should not be entitled to any right. My answer to this objection is that a self's not-yet-existence makes no moral difference in the attribution of rights to her, as I show in the following example. If somebody injects the virus of a fatal disease into an individual's body, the right to life of the individual (or, we can say, of the individual's present self) is violated. If the individual is injected with a variant of the fatal virus that has a long latency without any symptoms and she will die in 15 years' time, this injection is a violation of her future self's right to life, even though her future self is not present at the time the virus is injected.[12] I do not consider the time at which the virus activates to be morally relevant in ascribing rights to the individual's diachronic selves. One's present and future selves do not have morally different statuses. On the basis of the same reasoning, I contend that the normative force of the right to an open present does not decrease as a person ages. As long as a person is an agent, she has a set of normative principles to pursue. As aging occurs, a person may have less energy and less time ahead of her in which to realize her projects, but these conditions do not reduce her right to pursue her set of normative principles.

It is possible that an individual's future self will not come to exist, if the individual dies prematurely. Thus, it can be objected that, by respecting the obligation to preserve the future self's agency, the present self limits her freedom in favor of an agent who may not come into existence. Uncertainty about our future existence affects every aspect of our mortal life. In synchronic moral relationships with other individuals, we face the same issues: our moral commitments toward them could be interrupted by our own or their deaths. However, in our everyday deliberations with other people, we act *as if* we and the other parties had normal lifespans. I suggest a similar reasoning for the diachronic self-regarding right that I am considering: the present self owes to the future self an open present and acts as if the future self will exist.

3.2 The intrapersonal nonidentity problem in the Moral Theory of Prudence

The nonidentity problem is usually treated as an interpersonal issue typical of intergenerational ethics (Schwartz 1978; Kavka 1981; Parfit 1984, ch. 16; 2017; Woodward 1986; Boonin 2014). It consists in the paradox of simultaneously holding the *person-affecting* view and the comparative notion of harm. According to the person-affecting view, an act is wrong, or at least worse than another, only if there is at least one person for whom the act makes things worse or if there is at least one person harmed by that act. The comparative notion of harm holds that an act bringing a person into existence whose life is worth living but flawed and who would have never existed without that act is an act that does not make things worse for or harm that person (Roberts 2020).

The future self's indeterminacy seems to give rise to an *intrapersonal nonidentity problem*: the action of an individual's present self that determines the beginning of the future self's coming into existence and that could be judged as putatively harmful to the future self (because the future self's life is worth living but flawed) is not harmful (Andersen 2021; Das and Paul 2020). Andersen (2021) discusses Fleurbaey's (1995) example of Bert, a motorcyclist who did not wear a helmet, had an accident, and became a numerically different person after the accident (called "post-accident Bert"). Andersen holds that this act is not harmful because post-accident Bert exists because of this act and, if his life is still worth living, he cannot be worse off than he otherwise would be because, if Bert had not refused to wear a helmet, post-accident Bert would not have existed. In other words, the act did not harm anyone.

It may seem that an intrapersonal non-identity problem affects a kind of diachronic self-regarding decision. This is the case in which the individual's present self makes a diachronic self-regarding decision entailing a personal transformative experience that brings about a future self numerically different from the present self and who has a flawed existence that is nonetheless worth living. From the perspective of the Moral Theory of Prudence, making such a decision violates the future self's right to an open present—and thus is morally wrong—if the decision undermines one or more necessary conditions for the pursuit of the future self's set of normative principles. However, according to the intrapersonal nonidentity problem, such a decision of the present self is never morally wrong, since without that decision the future self would not have existed.

My reply is that the nonidentity problem applies to the metaphysical level of reality; thus, it would undermine my theory only if the selves of my minimal, realistic model of the agent were conceived of as metaphysical entities. I treat the selves of diachronic self-regarding decisions as if they were numerically distinct and concede that the two selves of a person are numerically distinct in cases of change in the core normative principles. However, I always adopt this reading at the practical level (i.e., in the sphere of action). Hence, the Moral Theory of Prudence sidesteps the nonidentity problem because it deals with practical, not metaphysical, identities. As seen, the selves of my minimal, realistic model can be conceived as morally relevant attributes of a person.[13]

3.3 The alleged impossibility of an obligation toward oneself

In the Moral Theory of Prudence, the present self's requirement to preserve the future self's agency is an obligation that concerns one's diachronic selves. This obligation may be interpreted as a duty to oneself and thus be subject to the typical objection moved to such duties. Kant has provided the best known account of duties to oneself, in which duties to oneself are impersonal and impartial rules of action that pertain to the respect for our own humanity (Kant 1991 [1797], 6:417–47: 214–42). It is noteworthy that the similarity between Kantian duties to oneself and the obligation to preserve the future self's agency is partial. In fact, Kantian duties to oneself do not descend from prudence but from morality—more precisely, from the respect for humanity (Kant 1991 [1797], 6:420: 216). In my theory, the obligation to preserve the future self's agency is a requirement of both prudence and morality, as it is a moral requirement of prudence.

The objection to duties to oneself can take two forms. The first consists of contending that a moral duty or obligation is owed by an individual (the subject of the duty) to somebody (the object of the duty), who is numerically distinct from the individual and is the only one who can release the individual from the duty. As a consequence, since, in the case of duties to oneself, one (as the object of the duty) can release oneself (as the subject of the duty) from the duty, duties to oneself are easily waivable and thus cannot be duties; they lack the normative force of moral obligations (Singer 1959).

My answer to the first form of the objection against obligations to oneself is based on Schofield's (2015) position in the debate on duties to oneself. In the case of a diachronic self-regarding obligation, such as the obligation to preserve the future self's agency, a person's earlier self owes a duty to a later self that is not waivable, as only the later self could release the earlier self from the obligation, and this release is not possible because the later self is yet to come when the duty must be fulfilled (Schofield 2015, 516).[14] Thus, the temporal division of a person into diachronic selves sidesteps the objection.

The second form of the objection to duties to oneself consists of contending that duties to oneself concern one's happiness or well-being and thus are part of prudence and not morality (Baier 1958, 215). As several authors indicate (Kaspar 2011, 313; Hills 2003, 131; Neblett 1969, 71), this position is based on the view that prudence and morality are opposed and that morality is usually other-regarding.[15]

My answer to the second form of the objection against obligations to oneself derives from my conception of prudence as part of morality. I conceive of prudence as care for oneself, and I contend that such care is moral because it avoids some forms of harm to the future self and entails a moral relationship with oneself composed of the normative requirements of justifying one's action to oneself and protecting one's future agency. For this reason, I consider prudence as belonging to self-regarding morality. In addition, the obligation to give the future self an open present is grounded in agency, not well-being, as I discuss in section 3.5.[16]

3.4 The challenge of identity changes to backward-looking self-regarding responsibility and the irrelevance of forward-looking self-regarding responsibility

In Parfit's approach to personal identity, when the psychological connection between the present and future selves is weak, they are two distinct and independent entities, and the latter can thus be considered less or not responsible for the former's actions. A similar conclusion seems to derive from my account of practical identity in cases in which an individual's present and future selves have different core normative principles of action. It may be objected that when one's present and future selves are numerically distinct, my theory would not be agnostic regarding whether the future self has backward-looking self-regarding responsibility; my theory would rather contend that the future self has no such a responsibility. I reply that, even in such a case, the Moral Theory of Prudence is silent because it cannot be excluded that backward-looking self-regarding responsibility is tied to a different kind of identity (for instance, metaphysical identity) and thus can be inherited from one's earlier self by one's later self, even if the two selves are numerically distinct at the practical level.

An objection that may arise against the present self's forward-looking self-regarding responsibility is that such a responsibility is needless because it is self-evident that a person's present self is accountable for her actions affecting her future self. My answer is that the attribution of this responsibility is clear within an account of personal identity that considers the self as temporally extended to a person's life. However, in my model of practical identity, the future and present selves are considered as if they were numerically distinct and are actually numerically distinct in the case of changes of one's of core normative values; thus, forward-looking self-regarding responsibility needs to be justified.

3.5 Synthesis of the Moral Theory of Prudence in light of my replies to the main objections

The Moral Theory of Prudence regulates the relationship between one's present and future selves. It holds that one's present self has a moral obligation in the present to respect the future self's agency—that is, the future self's capacity or freedom (I use the terms interchangeably) to pursue her normative principles of actions—compatibly with the present self's capacity or freedom to pursue her normative principles. Such a moral obligation is grounded in the equal moral worth of all the selves—*qua* agents—of a person, regardless of their temporal position in this person's life. As both the present and future selves are entitled to pursue their own set of normative principles, the obligation to preserve the future self's agency does not favor the future self over that of the present self. Rather, it makes their conditions of agency the same.

The obligation to preserve the future self's agency and the right to an open present are reminiscent of the Kantian respect of persons, whom Kant conceives essentially in terms of agency: rational autonomous agents (Kant 2006 [1785], 4:427–28: 36–37, 4:436–37: 43–44, 4:446–47: 52, 4:452–53: 57). Yet I do not conceive the subjects of the present-self–future-self relationship as metaphysical persons. Rather, the selves of my account are practical agents similar to Parfit's characterization of the metaphysical person, which, in turn, resembles Hume's concept of the subject as a stream of experiences, thoughts, and actions (Hume 1928 [1738–1740], I.iv.6: 251–53). The similarity of my model of the agent to the Parfitian characterization of the person and the Humean subject lies in the fact that, in my model, a person's self cares for the person's successive self as a function of her perceived continuity with the latter. As my model of the agent does not make assumptions at the metaphysical level, it is not subject to the intrapersonal nonidentity problem and cannot attribute backward-looking self-regarding responsibility to the future self. The Moral Theory of Prudence can only establish that a person's present self has forward-looking self-regarding responsibility to her future self for the consequences of the present self's actions on the future self, as the present self satisfies the three conditions for the attribution of such a responsibility.

The Moral Theory of Prudence is a theory of respect for the agency of the diachronic selves. It is thus an *agency-centered* theory of prudence.

The novelty of my theory consists in temporally fragmenting the person in selves and analyzing the relationship among such selves through a moral framework that is based on a fundamental Kantian element: the respect for agency.

4. Alternative solutions to diachronic self-regarding decisions and their differences from the Moral Theory of Prudence

In this section, I present and discuss contemporary approaches to diachronic self-regarding decisions and diachronic self-regarding conflicts, the latter of which are diachronic self-regarding decisions in which one's present and future selves disagree on the best course of action.[17] The discussion of alternative solutions to diachronic self-regarding decisions comes after the presentation of my theory because this section order highlights the novelty of my approach and its theoretical basis. In this section, I focus on the differences between my theory and the alternatives; I only sketch or indicate in the notes the problems internal to each theory that do not pertain to the present-self–future-self relationship and the model of the agent.

4.1 Cureton, Bruckner, and Arvan: Contractarian approaches to diachronic self-regarding decisions

Inspired by Rawls' imaginary original position, some authors have provided contractarian accounts of diachronic self-regarding decisions. In an intrapersonal original position, the time slices (i.e., the diachronic selves) of an individual must agree on some principles of prudence under a veil of ignorance, which each author characterizes differently (Cureton 2016; Bruckner 2003, 2004; Arvan 2020).[18]

Cureton (2016) puts forth a partial framework of prudence for cases of identity crisis, in which someone suddenly loses values, loyalties, and commitments with which she used to identify and cannot replace them. An unexpected severe disability is an example of identity crisis (Cureton 2016, 816). In these cases, according to Cureton, the prudent action is the one that conforms to a plan of life that would be selected through a procedure in which one of the diachronic selves that is part of an individual's life takes up a hypothetical perspective. The aim of the procedure is to select from a finite list of possible life plans, one that is acceptable to all of an individual's selves. The self in the hypothetical perspective has access to counterfactual information and thus knows the kinds of selves that will result from the various life plans; she also knows empirical facts about human nature and some aspect of the individual of which she is part (e.g., her ethnicity, genetic make-up, desires, psychological tendencies). Cureton's hypothetical perspective is based on *objective rationality*. The latter specifies what the individual should do in light of all relevant facts about a situation, including those which the individual is not aware of at the moment of the choice. Thus, Cureton's theory of prudence for cases of identity crisis is an objective theory of prudence.

To avoid partiality, Cureton establishes that the self in the hypothetical perspective does not know the values, preferences, talents, and so on that she will have in the individual's life and the period of the individual's life in which the self will exist (Cureton 2016, 830–31). According to Cureton, the self adopting the hypothetical perspective would choose the life plan that maximizes the average weighted utility among all selves and enables the basic minimum satisfaction of all selves (Cureton 2016, 835).

The main problem with Cureton's contractarian approach is that he assumes a model of the agent that is too far from reality. The idealized self of Cureton's prudential original position possesses the pieces of information that a real or normal self does not: the idealized self, but not the real one, knows the possible and actual future selves of the person of whom she is part, as well as the life plans that are available. Accordingly, Cureton's approach is not easy to implement in real-life diachronic self-regarding decisions and assumes epistemic conditions that the real agent does not fulfill. From the individual's perspective, the epistemic impossibility of knowing the nature of her future self is one of the major features of diachronic self-regarding decisions. The individual possesses only *subjective reasons*, namely, claims about what she has reason to do, given her beliefs and information about her situation. Cureton affirms that his objective theory of prudence can be extended to a subjective theory of prudence by adding restrictions to the information possessed by the agent in the prudential original position (Cureton 2016, 816, 831). However, the problem is that a plausible, real agent has less information about the future selves of the person of whom she is part but at the same time has more information about herself than the idealized self of the prudential original position. In fact, the idealized self in Cureton's hypothetical perspective lacks the pieces of information that the real agent possesses, as the real but not the idealized self knows her values, preferences, and temporal position throughout the individual's life.

My Moral Theory of Prudence is not affected by the problem of the idealized agent, as it is founded only on the essential components of agency that every possible future self will possess. In addition, the model of the agent that my theory adopts is realistic in that it is based on empirical findings on the individual's perception of the future self.[19] As the individual's limited knowledge of her future self's plans, values, preferences, and so on is a fundamental characteristic of the present-self–future-self relationship, I do not abstract from this aspect and I do not aim to provide a theory of prudence based on objective rationality. Such a theory would not help a real individual facing a diachronic self-regarding decision. The individual's perspective of deliberation is that of *subjective rationality*—namely, it is the individual's concrete perspective, which includes the beliefs and information that she possesses when she makes the decision. As indicated by Williams, this is the perspective "from now" (Williams 1981a, cit., 13) and "from here" (Williams 1981b, cit., 35). My approach to prudence is based on subjective rationality and thus provides a subjective theory of prudence.

Bruckner (2003, 2004) proposes that, in cases of diachronic self-regarding conflicts, prudence requires the *minimax regret principle*: taking the action whose associated maximum level of regret is the smallest. The minimax regret principle is derived from how Bruckner devises the intrapersonal original position. In the latter, each time slice of a person (i.e., each diachronic self) must decide for the principle of prudence that best secures her interests; each self knows general facts about human nature (2003, 37, 2004, 47), but not her own preferences and the time at which she will exist, nor her possible life plans and counterfactual information related to these plans. Moreover, in Bruckner's prudential original position, each time slice of a person wants to avoid regret for the losses she could have imposed on the person's earlier time slices and could impose on the person's later time slices. Bruckner demonstrates that the more individuals care for their later and earlier selves, the more the minimax regret principle converges with the principle of expected aggregate utility maximization (Bruckner 2003, 44).

Arvan (2020) proposes a theory of prudence based on an intrapersonal contract that is not subject to the objection of the idealized agent because the selves of his intrapersonal original position are characterized by the moral psychology revealed by neurobehavioral evidence. His theory of prudence concerns being prudent in life in general; he touched upon on diachronic self-regarding decisions when dealing with the *problem of possible future selves*, namely self- and other-regarding decisions in which the agent wants to know if she will regret her decisions in the future but she cannot know that as she cannot know the future (Arvan 2016, 47–51, 2020, 61).

As said in Chapter 2,[20] in Arvan's theory, prudence means acting in ways that have the best expected lifetime utility for the agent in terms of achieving her ends (Arvan 2020, 26–28, 51) and is founded on the individual's internalization of moral risk aversion (Arvan 2020, ch. 2). An individual's moral risk aversion has the same effect on her decision-making as Bruckner's minimax regret principle (Bruckner 2003): choosing actions that minimize the maximum possible amount of regret.

According to Arvan, the Categorical-Instrumental Imperative is the best strategy for minimizing the maximum possible amount of regret. The Categorical-Instrumental Imperative consists of the principle commanding the individual to act on chosen interests upon which all of an individual's diachronic selves agree, regardless of how the past and future might turn out and what interests the past, present, and future selves could possibly have (Arvan 2020, 63–64). This means that, as it is possible that one's future self may develop interests for other human and nonhuman sentient beings, a contract among one's selves in this intrapersonal original position should include such interests (Arvan 2020, 64–65). The Categorical-Instrumental Imperative thus enables one to solve the problem of multiple future selves and to be fair to oneself, as all possible interests of a person's selves are equally taken into account.

Like Arvan, I employ a realistic model of the agent based on empirical findings[21] and consider prudence as moral.[22] Arvan affirms that the nature and persistence of agents is a metaphysical issue that does not involve normative theorizing (Arvan 2020, 27). However, while I agree that the metaphysical level of the entity facing diachronic self-regarding decisions is not relevant for investigating prudence, I add that, as prudence is care for oneself, it involves understanding this "oneself" at the practical level—that is, the sphere of the individual's actions.[23] Therefore, I contend that an account of prudence requires indicating who the relevant entities that make decisions are.

Arvan's solution and my solution to the problem of multiple selves are based on a similar reasoning. Arvan elaborates a normative principle of prudence (i.e., the Categorical-Instrumental Imperative) that is intrapersonally universal in the sense that it protects every possible interest that one's future selves will develop (Arvan 2016, 111–15, 2020, 64). I found two normative principles of prudence (i.e., the right to an open present and the obligation to preserve the future self's agency) on a component that any possible future self has, namely the normative principles of actions. In both approaches, what the selves pursue (interests or normative principles) is respected without specifying it (because this is not possible, as, in the present, one cannot know her future self's interests or normative principles).

There is a main difference between Arvan's approach and my own. It lies in the arguments supporting the thesis that prudence is moral. I consider prudence as moral because I conceive it as a subset of morality concerning one's moral relation with herself.[24] By contrast, Arvan derives morality from prudence by arguing that, in order to avoid future possible regret, the individual must act on interests that include other human and nonhuman sentient beings because one's future self may be interested in them.

4.2 Brink and McKerlie: Conflicts of values among diachronic selves

Like Cureton, Brink (2003) adopts the perspective of objective rationality to solve diachronic self-regarding conflicts. Brink proposes a solution based on temporal neutrality (i.e., the requirement that one should have equal concern for one's diachronic selves) and objective reasons, namely, claims about what the individual has reason to do, given the facts of her situation—regardless of whether she is aware of these facts. He deals with diachronic self-regarding conflicts in which one's earlier and later selves have different values or ideals, meant as Nagel's "principles about what things *constitute* reason for actions" (Nagel 1970, cit., 74, italics in the original). He does not treat such conflicts as interpersonal or interagential because he contends that, in normal cases of diachronic self-regarding conflicts of values, the individual after the change of value (called *After*) is still psychologically connected to the one before the change (called *Before*). Thus, Before and After are the same individual. According to Brink, it is usually Before that voluntarily started the change. This deliberative control of the change psychologically connects After and Before and makes the change not substantial (Brink 2003, 232–23).[25]

Brink suggests solving diachronic self-regarding conflicts by examining the merits of Before's and After's values from the perspective of objective rationality. Therefore, if Before's values are more worthy than After's values, Before—who is the agent facing the diachronic self-regarding conflict (i.e., the present self in my account)—should follow her current values. If After's values are more worthy than Before's, Before should follow After's values. As Brink admits, this is not rational from the perspective of subjective rationality: Before is required to act on reasons provided by values that she does not hold at the time of the decision.

McKerlie (2007) puts forth a different solution based on objective rationality to conflicts of values without the individual's change of identity. His solution combines the principle of maximizing one's well-being with two views about well-being: the assumption that some values are objectively more important than other values and the *positive response condition*. The positive response condition states that the positive response is a determinant of well-being that consist of one's positive reaction, which comes in degrees, to a valuable state or activity, such as desiring or enjoying a state or activity (McKerlie 2007, 64). In McKerlie's approach, two issues should be assessed in a conflict between the values of one's present self and those of the future self: first, which option achieves the goal that is the most valuable from an objective perspective; and second, whether and how much one will respond positively to the effects of the option selected, when she will experience them. If she does not respond positively to an option, the latter does not maximize one's well-being and thus should not be taken (McKerlie 2007, 65).

Neither Brink nor McKerlie deals with the appropriate characterization of the individual's epistemic situation for determining the individual's subjective reasons.[26] Brink admits that the requirements of temporal neutrality and the objective reasons converge with the agent's subjective reasons only in some cases of diachronic self-regarding conflicts (Brink 2003, 237–38). As in real-life diachronic self-regarding decisions, the individual has a limited knowledge of her future self's values and conditions, both Brink's and McKerlie's solutions to diachronic self-regarding decisions are infeasible from the individual's perspective.[27]

4.3 Parfit: The discounted concern for one's future self

Parfit touches upon diachronic self-regarding decisions and conflicts of values when discussing the implications of his reductionist theory of personal identity on prudence and commitments (Parfit 1984, 317–19, 325–28). In Parfit's view, the individual facing diachronic self-regarding decisions is a Humean subject connected to the past and future parts of her life (i.e., the diachronic selves) through a stream of memories, intentions, beliefs, and desires. As seen in Chapter 2,[28] according to Parfit, when one's present self has enough psychological continuity or connectedness with one's future self (relation R), this relation gives the present self a reason to have special concern for the future self (Parfit 1984, 312). One's concern for the future self thus depends on the strength of relation R between one's earlier and later selves, therefore legitimating a discount rate of one's future utilities on the basis of the weakening of relation R (Parfit 1984, 313). This means that in case of a diachronic self-regarding decision, the prudential requirement demanded of the individual's present self depends on the strength of relation R with the future self. If the individual's present self has high psychological connection with the future self, then the present self should give significant weight to the claims coming from the future self. If the individual's present self has low psychological connection with the future self, then the present self should give reduced weight to the claims coming from the future self. For Parfit, in case the relation R between one's earlier and later selves is too weak or absent and the earlier self's values differ from the later self's, the latter cannot be forced to pursue the earlier self's values—for instance, by committing to a project of the earlier self (Parfit 1984, 325–28).

Although my minimal, realistic model of the agent takes into account the possible weakening of relation R between diachronic selves (i.e., the care for the future self of one's present self depends on the present self's perceived connection with the future self), I do not propose discounting one's care for her future self on the basis of the strength of that relation. One can attribute a weight to the right to an open present when deliberating about which action to take, but the outcome of one's deliberation is either that one respects this right (if the latter has the highest weight among the other moral considerations assessed) or that one does not respect it (if another moral consideration has a higher weight than the right to an open present).

It may be objected that, in a diachronic self-regarding decision, the option that leaves more opportunities open to the future self than the other option entails more care for the future self than the other one; in other words, this objection states that in my Moral Theory of Prudence, there are degrees of care for the future self like in Parfit's approach.[29] However, the obligation to protect the future self's agency does not regard the number of options that are left accessible to the future self but the necessary conditions for the pursuit of any set of normative principles. Such obligation requires choosing the option that does not jeopardize *all* necessary conditions. Therefore, an option (I call it O) that threatens *some* necessary conditions does not entail lower care for one's future self than one protecting all necessary conditions; O does not protect the future self, in the sense established by the Moral Theory of Prudence: O does not protect her agency. Thus, within my framework, we cannot say that one protects her future self's agency a little or a lot; either one protects it or she does not.

4.4 Pettigrew: Conflicts of changing selves

Pettigrew (2020) deals with diachronic self-regarding conflicts in which an individual's earlier and later selves are *changing selves*—that is, they are not numerically identical. He interprets the diachronic relationships among an individual's selves as interpersonal. Pettigrew conceives the person as a corporate entity that is constituted by her past, present, and future selves. The self facing a diachronic self-regarding decision is the chief executive officer (CEO) of the corporation. The CEO makes a decision on behalf of the corporation, namely, of all the selves (Pettigrew 2020, 49, 229). Pettigrew characterizes the individual's selves as agents who discount the utilities of the later selves as a function of their Parfitian relation R with the later selves (Pettigrew 2020, 160, 187). He affirms that this trait accounts for the individual's first-person perception of her future selves (Pettigrew 2020, 187), and I add that it is compatible with the empirical findings on the perception of one's future self.

Pettigrew reads diachronic self-regarding conflicts as problems of collective decision-making, which he aims to solve with the Aggregate Utility Solution: a theory of rational decision-making based on expected utility theory (Pettigrew 2020, 7). The Aggregate Utility Solution computes a person's utility as the weighted average of the utilities of her past, present, and future selves combined with the current self's credence function. Although Pettigrew does not tackle the relationship between prudence and morality, he indicates a moral constraint for the assignment of weights to the utilities of the various selves. This moral constraint is the current self's obligation to give some weight to the utilities of the past selves that made sacrifices for their later selves from which the current self benefits (Pettigrew 2020, 159, 167–83). For Pettigrew, in a diachronic self-regarding conflict with one's changing selves, the action to take is the one that maximizes a person's utility as computed with the Aggregate Utility Solution.

Although my Moral Theory of Prudence indicates some moral constraints to the present self, they are not related to the attribution of weights to the selves' utilities. My theory is based on agency and gives moral constraints directly to the present self's actions: choosing the action that protects the future self's agency, compatibly with enabling the present self to pursue her normative principles. Moreover, the requirement to attribute some weight to the past self's utilities in the case that the present self benefited from the past self's sacrifices may be read within the framework of my theory as a constraint on the future self's pursuit of her normative principles of action and thus a limitation of her open present. Certainly, if the future self wants to carry on a project initiated by the present self, this does not limit the future self's open present. However, if the future self is not interested in this project, the Moral Theory of Prudence states that the future self should not pursue it.

I agree with Pettigrew that a plausible model of the agent must take into account the empirical finding that one's interest in her later self varies as a function of her psychological connection with her later self. However, I argue that Pettigrew's approach has two issues. The first is the justification of the interpretation of the present-self–future-self relationship as interpersonal. If a diachronic self-regarding conflict is read as interpersonal, it should imply two numerically distinct persons, yet this does not seem the case in Pettigrew's theory. Pettigrew does not provide his view on the identity of the self or agent facing a diachronic self-regarding conflict. Without that view, it is not clear who a self is according to the Aggregate Utility Solution; consequently, it is not clear whether Pettigrew's theory can be better interpreted as interagential, namely, as stating that self-regarding diachronic conflicts are conflicts between two agents rather than two persons. On the one hand, Pettigrew's position on personal identity seems close to Parfit's view, as the self of Pettigrew's approach cares for later and earlier selves as a function of relation R (Pettigrew 2020, 160, 187, 212). On the other hand, Pettigrew's position on personal identity seems inscribable in the metaphysical view of the person as a unit, since the relevant entity of his Aggregate Utility Solution is the person (the corporation, in his theory) and not the selves, who are merely parts of this unit. Yet, as seen, a metaphysical concept of the person is not required when discussing diachronic self-regarding decisions.[30]

The second issue in Pettigrew's approach is the idealization of the agent. As an individual's present self needs to aggregate the utilities of the past and future selves, she needs to compare these utilities. To do so, Pettigrew assumes that the present self can compare, among other things, differences between the utilities of the same item at different times (namely, differences between the utility that she attributes to an outcome and the utilities that the other selves attribute to it) (Pettigrew 2020, 103). This capacity is very demanding for a real agent, especially when she needs to figure out the difference between her utility and the utilities of selves that are far in the past (and thus not easy to remember) or far in the future (and thus not easy to foresee).

4.5 Dorsey: Current self's sacrifice for a later or earlier self

Recently, Dorsey (2021) has provided a comprehensive account of prudential rationality. This account includes a subjectivist theory of prudential value, which holds that the person attributes value to what is good for her. Dorsey's account also indicates the demands of prudence in a context of temporal neutrality. Such an account is an objective theory of prudence because it is based on objective prudential reasons that abstract away from the agent's epistemic conditions (Dorsey 2021, 209). Thus, this account is subject to the objection of excessive idealization of the agent, whom Dorsey identifies in the person (Dorsey 2021, 243–44). I focus on the aspect of Dorsey's theory regarding a potential conflict between diachronic selves: specifically, the present self's sacrifice for a later or earlier self (Dorsey 2021, chs. 10, 12). Dorsey contends that such a sacrifice is legitimate and should be conceived of as a compensation because he assumes the traditional view on personal identity, according to which the person is a unit and the diachronic selves are not independent parts of, but rather contribute to, the latter (Dorsey 2021, 244). As Dorsey defends temporal neutrality, he holds that not only now-for-later but also now-for-earlier sacrifices are compensations (Dorsey 2021, 307).

Dorsey conceives of prudence as what is good for oneself (Dorsey 2021, 10) and understands prudence not in terms of well-being, but in terms of facts concerning prudential goods (Dorsey 2021, 14, 220–21). According to him, prudence requires maximizing one's good throughout one's life. More precisely, prudence demands that an individual conform to the strongest balance of her prudential reasons, where the strength of each prudential reason is determined by the value one attributes to the goods that ground the reasons at stake (Dorsey 2021, 216).

According to Dorsey, in a person's prudential ordering (i.e., the ordinal ranking of one's prudential values), the primary prudential values are her long-term projects. The fact that a particular good is a project is an intrinsic good-making factor that outweighs the non-project goods (Dorsey 2021, 157). The value of a successful completed project is higher than that of non-project goods. Dorsey attributes not only a prudential but also a non-prudential normative significance to projects, on the basis that being committed to a project is itself a normative fact (Dorsey 2021, 310). Projects require a commitment among the diachronic selves, as they take time to be accomplished (Dorsey 2021, 282). For Dorsey, even if one's present self no longer values a project started in the past, its completion benefits one's past self, who did value the project (Dorsey 2021, 248). Therefore, the upshot of Dorsey's theory is that prudence requires one's present self to complete even projects that one wants to abandon or repudiate and to lay the groundwork for future projects (Dorsey 2021, 281, 249, 301), if the past and future selves' benefits are greater than the present self's harm (Dorsey 2021, 307).

The requirement of Dorsey's theory of prudence is highly demanding and risks alienating one's present self from her own projects. Dorsey acknowledges this risk and replies with three arguments. First, the demandingness of a normative theory of prudence is not a reason for abandoning it (Dorsey 2021, 303). Second, the normative authority of prudence is limited: the commands of prudence are not all-things-considered requirements and thus can be flouted for various reasons (e.g., because of their demandingness or because of the overriding nature of moral requirements) (Dorsey 2021, 304, 308). Third, the prudential value of one's past and future projects can be outweighed by the non-prudential normative significance of current projects, which is independent of the prudential significance (Dorsey 2021, 308–9). Thus, in a conflict between pursuing one's present project and one's future project, it is possible that non-prudential normative (e.g., moral) reasons to pursue one's current project outweigh the prudential reasons to lay a basis for a future project (Dorsey 2021, 311).

The thesis that prudential requirements can be trumped by moral requirements implicitly assumes that the moral and prudential spheres are detached and that the moral sphere is more normatively authoritative than the prudential sphere. This thesis requires a clarification of how Dorsey conceives the relationship between morality and prudence and a justification of the assumption that the former is more authoritative than the latter.

In addition, Dorsey's approach does not acknowledge the possibility that a person's diachronic selves can be considered independent from each other at the practical level. Therefore, his theory cannot protect a person's later selves from decisions made by this person's earlier selves that reduce these later selves' agency. In fact, if the significant unit is the person, violating the right to an open present of any of this person's diachronic selves is simply seen as a sacrifice that is compensated for intrapersonally.

4.6 Comparison between the Moral Theory of Prudence and the alternative approaches

The Moral Theory of Prudence differs from the alternative approaches to diachronic self-regarding decisions in three respects. First, the discussion of the current approaches to diachronic self-regarding decisions highlights that several approaches (Cureton 2016; Arvan 2020; McKerlie 2007; Pettigrew 2020) provide a solution grounded in one's well-being, usually expressed in terms of utility. These approaches reduce diachronic self-regarding decisions to a matter of well-being, thus excluding other relevant factors. The basis of the Moral Theory of Prudence is precisely a factor that cannot be reduced to well-being: the agency of the individual's selves.

Grounding a theory of prudence on agency is made possible by my characterization of the subject taking actions. As I differentiate between the person as a metaphysical substance and the self or agent as the practical entity that acts in the practical sphere, I can conceive the relationships among diachronic selves as relationships among agents. Accordingly, the Moral Theory of Prudence interprets diachronic self-regarding decisions as interagential decisions. This is the second difference between the Moral Theory of Prudence and the alternative approaches, which interpret diachronic self-regarding decisions as intrapersonal (Cureton 2016; Bruckner 2003, 2004; Arvan 2020; Brink 2003; McKerlie 2007; Dorsey 2021) or interpersonal (Parfit 1984; Pettigrew 2020).

The third difference regards the distance between the real agent making diachronic self-regarding decisions and the model of the agent employed in these approaches. In many approaches to diachronic self-regarding decisions (Cureton 2016; Brink 2003; McKerlie 2007; Pettigrew 2020; Dorsey 2021), this distance is large: these approaches assume epistemic conditions that the real agent does not fulfill and/or cognitive capacities that she does not have. In contrast, the Moral Theory of Prudence is based on an empirically plausible model of the agent and her perspective in the here and now. It is thus a subjective theory of prudence.

Table 3.1 Summary of the alternative approaches to the Moral Theory of Prudence in diachronic self-regarding decisions with the cases that each approach regulates, the principle of prudence it requires, and the model of agent that it employs.

Author of the approach	Cases regulated	Normative principle	Model of agent
Cureton	Diachronic self-regarding decisions with identity crisis	Choosing the life guaranteeing the minimum satisfaction for all of an individual's diachronic selves and maximizing the average weighted utility among all selves	The agent is a person's time slice and is idealized, as she has access to counterfactual information, that is, she knows the kinds of selves that will result from the various life plans
Bruckner	Diachronic self-regarding conflicts	Minimax regret principle: choosing the action whose maximum level of regret is the smallest	The agent is a person's time slice that wants to avoid regret of the person's earlier and later time slices
Arvan	Being prudent in life (diachronic self-regarding decisions are tackled in the problem of possible future selves)	Categorical-Instrumental Imperative: acting on chosen interests upon which one's diachronic selves agree, which results in one's best expected lifetime utility	Realistic agent characterized by the moral psychology revealed in neurobehavioral studies
Brink	Diachronic self-regarding conflicts of values	Choosing the value that is more worthy from the perspective of objective rationality	Idealized agent who in the present knows her future values
McKerlie	Diachronic self-regarding conflicts of values without the individual's change of identity	Maximizing one's well-being, as determined by the objective value of states and activities and one's positive response	Idealized agent who in the present knows her future values

Author of the approach	Cases regulated	Normative principle	Model of agent
Parfit	Diachronic self-regarding decisions	Caring for one's future self in degrees depending on the strength of one's relation R	Humean subject connected to her past and future time slices through relation R
Pettigrew	Diachronic self-regarding conflicts with numerically different selves	Aggregate Utility Solution: choosing the action with the highest weighted average of the utilities of one's selves combined with the present self's credence function	Person as a corporate entity consisting of idealized diachronic selves who can compare the differences between outcome utilities of the various selves
Dorsey	Being prudent in life (diachronic self-regarding decisions are tackled in the current self's sacrifice for a later or earlier self)	Conforming to the strongest balance of prudential reasons, whose strength is determined by the value that one attributes to the goods grounding such reasons	Person as an idealized agent of which the diachronic selves are part

5. Conclusion

In this chapter, I elaborated a normative theory, namely, the Moral Theory of Prudence in diachronic self-regarding decisions, which should guide one's present self in such decisions. This theory is constituted of a set of requirements descending from the moral analysis of the features of the present-self–future-self relationship and based on a model of practical identity that treats one's present and future selves as distinct agents. The Moral Theory of Prudence attributes forward-looking self-regarding responsibility and the obligation to preserve the future self's agency to the present self. It ascribes the right to an open present to the future self and, in the case of identity change, justifies her use of the self-regarding veto power against the present self's projects.

While many approaches to diachronic self-regarding decisions are based on idealized models of the self that are too far from reality (Cureton 2016; Brink 2003; McKerlie 2007; Pettigrew 2020; Dorsey 2021), the Moral

Theory of Prudence is grounded in an empirically plausible model of agent. In addition, this theory interprets self-regarding decisions as interagential on the basis of the minimal, realistic model of the agent. Furthermore, unlike some existing approaches to diachronic self-regarding decisions (Cureton 2016; Arvan 2020; McKerlie 2007; Pettigrew 2020), the Moral Theory of Prudence is not grounded in well-being but in the agency of the selves.

In the next chapter, I illustrate how the Moral Theory of Prudence works in practice. I provide a first application of the theory to the Russian nobleman's diachronic self-regarding conflict, which is a case devised by Parfit (1984, 326–28). I then show what the Moral Theory of Prudence tells us in the case of advance healthcare directives.

Notes

1. If one's future self is no longer an agent—for instance, in the case of neurodegenerative diseases—the Moral Theory of Prudence does not apply, since in such cases we cannot truly refer to a future agent that may disagree with the decision made by the earlier self. I deal with such cases in the next chapter.
2. Here, I consider the diachronic self-regarding decisions of healthy individuals. Therefore, I exclude pathological cases in which the individual is affected by a psychological or mood disorder, such as depression, and thus experiences limited agency in the present.
3. See section 3.1.
4. In other words, in my approach, each diachronic self of a person is entitled to the same rights and duties toward the other selves. Therefore, the Moral Theory of Prudence ensures that each diachronic self of a person is treated fairly, in the sense of treated equally with respect to the other selves. I thank Markus Arvan for raising the issue of how my approach relates to fairness to oneself.
5. See section 3.1 for the relationship between my theory and the theories of rights.
6. See Chapter 2, section 4.
7. Authenticity is one of the two normative elements involved in self-regarding decisions (Chapter 2, section 1); the other normative element is prudence.
8. See Carter (2018) and Tomlin (2013) for two substantial theories on backward-looking responsibility within a framework of personal identity in which the agent does not necessarily temporally extend to the whole duration of the person's life of which she is part. Carter attributes backward-looking responsibility, which he calls *liability-responsibility*, to one's later self, even when the latter is numerically different from one's earlier self. This is because he holds that liability-responsibility of a person's self is passed to the successive proximate self through psychological connectedness. In contrast, Tomlin contends that, in a Parfitian reductionist approach to identity, it is relation R that matters for the attribution of responsibility. Thus, if one's present and future selves are weakly connected by relation R, the transference of responsibility is undermined.
9. See Chapter 2, section 2.3.
10. See Chapter 2, section 3.4.
11. In the will theory, having a right vis-à-vis another person means exercising power over that person's duty to act in certain ways (Hart 1955).

12. My example is an intrapersonal version of the intergenerational case of the bomb hidden in a kindergarten that will explode in six years and kill children who are not alive at the time the bomb is concealed (Feinberg 1984, 97).
13. See Chapter 2, section 3.1.
14. Schofield also affirms that, to demonstrate that duties to oneself are possible, it is not necessary that an individual have two numerically distinct selves. What is required is the acknowledgment that, throughout her life, a person or individual occupies many distinct temporal standpoints (Schofield 2015, 520), which are points of view from which she perceives and assesses the world (Schofield 2015, 517). Such temporal standpoints are similar to the diachronic selves of my model or practical identity: they are attributes of a person and belong to the practical, not metaphysical level.
15. See Chapter 2, section 2.1.
16. Hills (2003) considers duties to oneself as both moral and prudential requirements, but she grounds them on well-being. She contends that if we have moral reasons to promote people's well-being, we have moral reasons to promote our well-being, as duties are universal reasons that count for every agent, ourselves included. According to Hills, duties to promote one's own well-being are prudential because they are grounded in the importance of well-being; they are also moral because concern for somebody's well-being (where this somebody can also be one's own self) is moral.
17. Bykvist (2006) delineates a theory of prudence for a simplified version of choices in which the individual knows that the option that she chooses will change her preference about the choice options. I do not discuss this theory because Bykvist excludes diachronic conflicts between the individual's earlier and later selves from that simplified version.
18. Lenman (2009) gives a contractarian reading of care for oneself, contending that one's choice must be acceptable to each time slice of an individual, but he neither devises an original position nor derives principles of prudence from this position.
19. See Chapter 2, section 3.2.
20. See Chapter 2, section 2.2.
21. See Chapter 2, section 3.2.
22. See Chapter 2, sections 2.3 and 3.4.
23. See Chapter 2, section 3.1.
24. See also sections 2.3 and 3.4 of Chapter 2 and section 2.4 of this chapter.
25. An internal issue in Brink's approach is the impossibility of solving the diachronic self-regarding conflicts in which Before did not start the change—for example, exogenous events like a disability caused by a disease or a crisis conversion in which the change is felt as irresistible and not chosen (Ullmann-Margalit 2006, 161–62). In such cases, Before and After lack the psychological link constituted by the deliberative control of the change.
26. McKerlie rejects a subjective theory of prudence because he affirms that the latter is likely reducible to the present-aim theory, which is the view that a person should act on her present values in a diachronic self-regarding conflict (McKerlie 2007, 72). As shown by McKerlie, the present-aim theory presents a main inconsistency. The theory requires that the individual should decide only on the basis of her present values. Once a diachronic self-regarding conflict is past, the result of the requirement of the present-aim theory is that the life of the current present self (i.e., who was the future self when the conflict was in the present) is determined by the earlier self's values that were expressed in the past

decision, which the current present self may no longer hold (McKerlie 2007, 58). However, a subjective theory of prudence does not necessarily equate with the present-aim theory: the fact that the present self does not know her future self's values does not imply that she is required to act only on her present aims. A subjective theory of prudence can put some constraints on the present self's actions precisely because of her objective ignorance.
27. McKerlie's approach also presents two internal issues: first, the solution is vulnerable to the positions on well-being that do not accept value objectivism and the positive response; second, McKerlie's statement that only simultaneous and retrospective positive responses contribute to well-being is also controversial (see Bykvist (2007)).
28. See Chapter 2, section 2.2.
29. I thank Markus Arvan for raising this objection.
30. See Chapter 2, section 3.1.

References

Andersen, Didde Boisen. 2021. "I Have Got a Personal Non-Identity Problem: On What We Owe Our Future Selves." *Res Publica* 27 (July): 129–44. https://doi.org/10.1007/s11158-020-09474-0.
Arvan, Marcus. 2016. *Rightness as Fairness: A Moral and Political Theory*. New York: Palgrave Macmillan.
———. 2020. *Neurofunctional Prudence and Morality*. New York: Routledge.
Baier, Kurt. 1958. *The Moral Point of View: A Rational Basis of Ethics*. Ithaca, NY: Cornell University Press.
Beckerman, Wilfred, and Joanna Pasek. 2001. *Justice, Posterity and the Environment*. Oxford: Oxford University Press.
Boonin, David. 2014. *The Non-Identity Problem and the Ethics of Future People*. Oxford: Oxford University Press. https://doi.org/10.1007/s10677-015-9614-4.
Brink, David O. 2003. "Prudence and Authenticity: Intrapersonal Conflicts of Value." *Philosophical Review* 112 (2): 215–45. https://doi.org/10.1215/00318108-112-2-215.
Bruckner, Donald W. 2003. "A Contractarian Account of (Part of) Prudence." *American Philosophical Quarterly* 40 (1): 33–46. https://doi.org/10.2307/20010095.
———. 2004. "Prudence and Justice." *Economics and Philosophy* 20 (1): 35–63. https://doi.org/10.1017/S0266267104001257.
Bykvist, Krister. 2003. "The Moral Relevance of Past Preferences." In *Time and Ethics: Essays at the Intersection*, edited by H. Dyke, 115–36. Dordrecht: Springer. https://doi.org/10.1007/978-94-017-3530-8_9.
———. 2006. "Prudence for Changing Selves." *Utilitas* 18 (3): 264–83. https://doi.org/10.1017/S0953820806002032.
———. 2007. "Comments on Dennis McKerlie's 'Rational Choice, Changes in Values Over Time, and Well-Being.'" *Utilitas* 19 (1): 73–77.
Carter, Ian. 2018. "Equal Opportunity, Responsibility, and Personal Identity." *Ethical Theory and Moral Practice* 21: 825–39. https://doi.org/10.1007/s10677-018-9901-y.
Cureton, Adam. 2016. "Prudence and Responsibility to Self in an Identity Crisis." *Res Philosophica* 93 (4): 815–41. https://doi.org/10.11612/resphil.1466.

Das, Nilanjan, and Laurie Ann Paul. 2020. "Transformative Choice and the Non-Identity Problem." In *Derek Parfit's Reasons and Persons*, edited by A. Sauchelli, 187–208. London: Routledge. https://doi.org/10.4324/9780429488450-12.

De George, Richard T. 1981. "The Environment, Rights, and Future Generations." In *Responsibilities to Future Generations*, edited by E. Partridge. New York: Prometheus Books.

Dorsey, Dale. 2021. *A Theory of Prudence*. Oxford University Press. https://doi.org/10.1093/oso/9780198823759.001.0001.

Feinberg, Joel. 1984. *Harm to Others. The Moral Limits of the Criminal Law*. New York: Oxford University Press. https://doi.org/10.1093/0195046641.001.0001.

———. 1992. "The Child's Right to an Open Future." In *Freedom and Fulfilment: Philosophical Essays*. Princeton: Princeton University Press. https://doi.org/10.4324/9781315633794.

Fleurbaey, Marc. 1995. "Equal Opportunity or Equal Social Outcome?" *Economics and Philosophy* 11 (1): 25–55. https://doi.org/10.1017/S0266267100003217.

Hart, Herbert L. A. 1955. "Are There Any Natural Rights?" *The Philosophical Review* 64 (2): 175–91.

Hills, Alison. 2003. "Duties and Duties to the Self." *American Philosophical Quarterly* 40 (2): 131–42. https://doi.org/10.2307/20010107.

Hume, David. 1928 [1738–1740]. *A Treatise of Human Nature*. Edited by L. A. Selby-Bigge. Oxford: Clarendon Press.

Jonas, Hans. 1984. *The Imperative of Responsibility: In Search of an Ethics for the Technological Age*. Chicago and London: University of Chicago Press.

Kant, Immanuel. 1991 [1797]. *The Metaphysics of Morals*. Edited by M. Gregor. *Kant: The Metaphysics of Morals*. Cambridge: Cambridge University Press. https://doi.org/10.1017/9781316091388.

———. 2006 [1785]. *Groundwork of the Metaphysics of Morals*. Edited by M. J. Gregor. Cambridge: Cambridge University Press.

Kaspar, D. 2011. "Can Morality Do Without Prudence?" *Philosophia* 39: 311–26.

Kavka, Gregory S. 1981. "The Paradox of Future Individuals." *Philosophy & Public Affairs* 11 (2): 93–112.

Lenman, James. 2009. "The Politics of the Self: Stability, Normativity and the Lives We Can Live with Living." In *Philosophy and Happiness*, edited by L. Bortolotti. London: Palgrave Macmillan.

Macklin, Ruth. 1981. "Can Future Generations Correctly Be Said to Have Rights?" In *Responsibilities to Future Generations*, edited by E. Partridge. New York: Prometheus.

McKerlie, Dennis. 2007. "Rational Choice, Changes in Values Over Time, and Well-Being." *Utilitas* 19 (1): 51–72. https://doi.org/10.1017/S0953820806002342.

Nagel, T. 1970. *The Possibility of Altruism*. Oxford: Oxford University Press.

Neblett, William. 1969. "Morality, Prudence, and Obligations to Oneself." *Ethics* 80 (1): 70–73. https://doi.org/10.1086/291752.

Noorman, Merel. 2020. "Computing and Moral Responsibility." In *The Stanford Encyclopedia of Philosophy*, edited by E. N. Zalta. Accessed July 31, 2021. https://plato.stanford.edu/archives/win2016/entries/computing-responsibility/.

Nussbaum, Martha C. 2000. *Women and Human Development*. Cambridge: Cambridge University Press. https://doi.org/10.1017/cbo9780511841286.

———. 2006. *Frontiers of Justice: Disability, Nationality, Species Membership.* Cambridge: Harvard University Press.
Parfit, Derek. 1984. *Reasons and Persons.* Oxford: Clarendon Press.
———. 2017. "Future People, the Non-Identity Problem, and Person-Affecting Principles." *Philosophy and Public Affairs* 45 (2): 118–57. https://doi.org/10.1111/papa.12088.
Pettigrew, Richard. 2020. *Choosing for Changing Selves.* Oxford: Oxford University Press.
Poel, Ibo van de. 2011. "The Relation Between Forward-Looking and Backward-Looking Responsibility." In *Moral Responsibility: Beyond Free Will and Determinism*, edited by N. Vincent, Ibo van de Poel, and Jeroen van den Hoven, 27:37–52. Dordrecht: Springer. https://doi.org/10.1007/978-94-007-1878-4_3.
Rawls, John. 1999. *A Theory of Justice: Revised Edition.* Cambridge: Belknap Press. https://doi.org/10.1080/713659260.
———. 2001. *Justice as Fairness: A Restatement.* Edited by E. Kelly. Cambridge and London: Harvard University Press.
Roberts, Melinda A. 2020. "The Nonidentity Problem." In *Stanford Encyclopedia of Philosophy,* edited by E. N. Zalta. Accessed July 31, 2021. https://plato.stanford.edu/archives/win2020/entries/nonidentity-problem/
Schofield, Paul. 2015. "On the Existence of Duties to the Self (and Their Significance for Moral Philosophy)." *Philosophy and Phenomenological Research* 90 (3): 505–28. https://doi.org/10.1111/phpr.12034.
Schwartz, Thomas. 1978. "Obligations to Posterity." In *Obligations to Future Generations*, edited by R. Sikora and B. Barry. Philadelphia: Temple University Press.
Sen, Amartya. 1979. "Equality of What? Tanner Lecture on Human Values." In *Tanner Lectures on Human Values*, edited by S. McMurrin. Cambridge: Cambridge University Press.
———. 1999. *Development As Freedom.* Oxford: Oxford University Press.
———. 2009. *The Idea of Justice.* London: Allen Lane.
Singer, Marcus G. 1959. "On Duties to Oneself." *Ethics* 69 (3): 202–5. https://doi.org/10.1086/291210.
Talbert, Matthew. 2019. "Moral Responsibility." In *Stanford Encyclopedia of Philosophy*, edited by E. N. Zalta. Accessed July 31, 2021. https://plato.stanford.edu/entries/moral-responsibility/
Tomlin, Patrick. 2013. "Choices Chance and Change: Luck Egalitarianism Over Time." *Ethical Theory and Moral Practice* 16 (2): 393–407. https://doi.org/10.1007/s10677-012-9340-0.
Ullmann-Margalit, Edna. 2006. "Big Decisions: Opting, Converting, Drifting." *Royal Institute of Philosophy Supplement* 58: 157–72.
Williams, Bernard. 1981a. "Moral Luck." In *Moral Luck: Philosophical Papers 1973–1980.* Cambridge: Cambridge University Press.
———. 1981b. "Persons, Character and Morality." In *Moral Luck: Philosophical Papers 1973–1980.* Cambridge: Cambridge University Press.
Woodward, James. 1986. "The Non-Identity Problem." *Ethics* 96 (4): 804–31. https://doi.org/10.1086/292801.

4 How does the Moral Theory of Prudence work in practice? The application of the theory to advance healthcare directives in dementia

1. Introduction

In the previous chapter, I elaborated the Moral Theory of Prudence, which regulates the relationship between one's present and future selves in diachronic self-regarding decisions. It is based on a model of practical identity concerning one's diachronic selves, namely, the minimal, realistic model of the agent (for this reason, I use the terms "agent" and "self" interchangeably), and the moral features of the present-self–future-self relationship. The theory holds that a person's present self has forward-looking self-regarding responsibility to her future self and the obligation to preserve the future self's agency (i.e., to preserve the necessary conditions for the future self's pursuit of her normative principles of actions). In addition, the theory attributes the right to an open present (i.e., the claim to pursue one's set of normative principles) to one's future self and, in the case of identity change (i.e., change of one's core normative principles), justifies the future self's use of self-regarding veto power. The requirements of the Moral Theory of Prudence are both moral and prudential because the theory is founded on the thesis that prudence is a moral requirement. It is an agency-centered theory: it regulates the relationship among the diachronic selves of a person through a moral framework that is based on respect for agency.

The Moral Theory of Prudence differs from the current approaches to diachronic self-regarding decisions in three ways. First, it does not provide a solution grounded in well-being but rather agency. Second, it conceives the relationships among diachronic selves as relationships among agents, and diachronic self-regarding decisions as interagential. Third, it does not assume epistemic conditions that the real agent does not fulfill and/or cognitive capacities she does not have.

In this chapter, I show what the Moral Theory of Prudence requires in practice by applying it first to Parfit's thought experiment of the nineteenth-century Russian nobleman, which is a diachronic self-regarding conflict. I then apply it to the case of advance healthcare directives (henceforth, advance directives) in the case of dementia. In dementia, patients are subject to changes in preferences, values, and personality that are expressed in words or behavior. These changes increase the likelihood that the interests of the patient with dementia conflict with those previously expressed in her advance directive. The classic example of such a conflict is that of a patient with dementia enjoying a life of simple fulfillments that her earlier self rejected by drawing up an advance directive limiting, in the case of dementia, her future self's duration of life or medical treatments. So long as the patient subject to an advance directive is an agent or presumed as such, advance directives are diachronic self-regarding decisions, and thus the Moral Theory of Prudence applies to them.

Advance directives are enforced when the patient is deemed incompetent (i.e., not able to make decisions). I focus on advance directives in dementia because, in such a disease, the patient does not drastically lose decision-making capacity and in some phases of the disease could still retain agency despite being declared incompetent. By means of my minimal, realistic model of the agent, I refute a main objection that is raised against the moral authority of advance directives: the *personal identity problem*. The personal identity problem states that, in some diseases such as dementia, the person writing the advance directive is numerically different from the patient subject to that directive as a result of significant psychological changes. Hence, the author of the advance directive cannot decide for another person (i.e., the subject of the directive). I contend that advance directives do not require the unity of personal identity over time to be valid. Rather, adjudicating their validity depends on whether the patient retains agency. Therefore, I suggest shifting the discussion from the metaphysical level of personal identity to the practical level of the agent.

2. A first application of the Moral Theory of Prudence: The nineteenth-century Russian nobleman

The nineteenth-century Russian nobleman is a famous diachronic self-regarding conflict in the philosophical literature. The Russian nobleman is a young socialist who, at a later age, will inherit land that he now wants to give to his peasants. He knows that in later age, he will become conservative and want to keep the land; thus, to realize his present socialist ideals, he signs a document that will force his later self to give away the inherited land. The document can be revoked by his wife, but he binds her through a promise never to permit revocation (Parfit 1984, 326–28).[1]

The Moral Theory of Prudence in practice 95

The conflict of the Russian nobleman is rather underspecified with regard to the identity relationship between the young and old noblemen. However, Parfit adds that the young nobleman regards his ideals as essential to his present self and thinks that their loss would cause him to cease to exist (Parfit 1984, 326). Parfit suggests that we may regard this case as interpersonal, as the young nobleman may be conceived as a numerically different person from the old nobleman. As already explained,[2] I do not take a stance on the identity conditions that make a person the same one over time as this is a long-debated metaphysical issue that does not need to be addressed when dealing with diachronic self-regarding conflicts. I rather analyze the Russian nobleman's case at the practical, and not metaphysical, level. In my minimal, realistic model of the agent, the young nobleman's ideals are part of the agent's core normative principles, and thus the identity criterion of the agent,[3] as they are fundamental principles characterizing him as that specific agent and, if they were lost, the young nobleman would consider himself as dead (Parfit 1984, 326). Therefore, I assume that the young and old noblemen are two numerically different selves of the same person; accordingly, I consider the Russian nobleman's case as an interagential conflict. We can imagine that the young Russian nobleman (A^0) becomes gradually cynical and conservative because of his life experiences and that, after, for instance, 40 years, the old Russian nobleman (A^{40}) will change his mind about giving his land to the peasants. It could be that A^{40} will change his opinion about the capacity of socialist ideals to improve the society, have a large family that needs to be economically supported, and consider this latter commitment more important than socialist ideals.

The case of the Russian nobleman is a diachronic self-regarding conflict with limited objective ignorance (the third feature of the present-self–future-self relationship),[4] as A^0 knows that A^{40} will exist and be conservative. The Moral Theory of Prudence states that A^{40} has the right to pursue his set of normative principles (e.g., family commitments), compatibly with A^0's pursuit of his own normative principles (i.e., advancing socialist ideals). If by giving his land to the peasants, A^0 has no other source of income, which is a necessary condition for the pursuit of any set of normative principles (and thus for enabling A^{40} to support his family, for instance), then A^0's document and agreement with his wife violate A^{40}'s right to an open present. If by giving his land to the peasants, A^0 has other sources of income, then A^0's document and agreement do not violate A^{40}'s right to an open present. Furthermore, donating the land is a way to realize socialist ideals but it is not the only one; for instance, A^0 could participate to political demonstrations or donate some money to the peasants to help them buy a land. Accordingly, keeping the land does not compromise A^0's pursuit of her normative principles. Thus, the Moral Theory of Prudence recommends A^0 not sign the document and make the agreement if donating the land irreversibly undermines A^{40}'s income, which is necessary for pursuing his set of normative principles. Moreover, A^{40}'s exercise of self-regarding veto power with regard to A^0's plan—namely, revoking A^0's will to give away the land—is justified: A^{40} has different core normative principles and hence would renounce to her agency and be inauthentic, if he realized A^0's plans.

Typical real-life diachronic self-regarding conflicts differ from the conflict faced by the Russian nobleman in that, at the time of the decision, the individual does not know whether her future self will exist, what her normative principles will be, and whether she will approve of the present self's decision. If we want to render the Russian nobleman's case more similar to actual diachronic self-regarding decisions, we must consider that decision from the perspective of the young nobleman's subjective rationality—that is, from the perspective of what he knows at the time of the decision. In this altered version of Parfit's thought experiment, the young nobleman does not know that his future self will become conservative and reject socialist ideals; he could only consider this possibility. What does the Moral Theory of Prudence therefore recommend to the young nobleman? The theory recommends that A^0 not sign the document and make the agreement with his wife if the land is the only source of income, since if he donated it to the peasants, A^{40} would lack a necessary condition for taking a life path different from that chosen by A^0.

3. Advance directives in dementia

3.1 Advance directives

Advance directives are statements in which a competent person provides directions for medical decisions regarding herself in the event that she becomes incompetent. Such instructions concern, for instance, the medical interventions that the person will refuse under specific conditions or her disposition on the termination of life support. Advance directives help caregivers and healthcare professionals make decisions for a patient when she cannot speak for herself (Jaworska 2017a).

Advance directives are important means of taking part in one's own future medical decision-making and thus exerting one's autonomy. The latter justifies the individual's authority to make a decision for her later self. Advance directives are a means of extending the agent's current normative principles of action into the future. They are a paradigmatic case of a choice in which one's present self decides for her future self, as they express an individual's will for her future medical treatment that consequently has a

The Moral Theory of Prudence in practice 97

direct impact on her future self's life and death. As long as a patient is an agent or presumed as such, advance directives can be considered diachronic self-regarding decisions. In the presence of one's earlier and later selves (i.e., one's earlier and later agents), we can view advance directives as diachronic self-regarding decisions. If agency cannot be attributed to the patient, advance directives are not diachronic self-regarding decisions between two agents because one is missing; there is only the agent before the medical condition.

3.2 Decision-making capacity and agency in dementia

As observed by Jaworska, advance directives work well in the cases for which they were first introduced in the law, such as persistent vegetative states. These are cases in which the individual has lost consciousness, cannot recover it, and does not express interests that could potentially conflict with those that she previously indicated in her advance directive (Jaworska 2017a). In medical contexts, decision-making capacity or competence (here, I use the terms interchangeably) refers to the ability to make medical decisions for oneself. A patient who lacks decision-making capacity is deemed incompetent; an individual in a persistent vegetative state is considered an incompetent patient.

A person's decision-making capacity enables her to lead her own life according to her normative principles of action. This is why, as stated by Buchanan and Brock (1989, 40–41), it is a serious moral issue to assess a person as incompetent while she still has decision-making capacity: doing so would deprive her of autonomy. In several medical conditions, such as dementia, the patient does not drastically but rather progressively loses decision-making capacity, and her interests may conflict with her previous will expressed in her instructions regarding medical treatments. Dementia is a collection of neurological conditions comprising memory decline, impairments in language and executive functions, personality changes, and loss of control of physical functions. It is classified as a neurocognitive disorder and it is more common in older people; its most common form is Alzheimer's disease (American Psychiatric Association 2013). In several forms of dementia, the patient's cognitive fluctuations (i.e., alterations of her cognition and attention for a period) render the assessment of her decision-making capacity more difficult, as her performances may vary significantly within a short period of time (Trachsel et al. 2015).

The concept of decision-making capacity currently used in medical research and practice is based exclusively on cognitive criteria. There are four components of decision-making capacity on which there is some consensus: expressing a choice, understanding, appreciation, and reasoning

(Grisso and Appelbaum 1998). Expressing a choice is the ability to communicate one's decision. Understanding is the ability to understand the meaning of relevant information. Appreciation is the ability to acknowledge how information applies to a person and her situation. Reasoning is the ability to reason about treatment choices, compare alternatives, and infer the consequences in a logical manner (Grisso and Appelbaum 1998, 34–58). One of the most used and validated tools for assessing decision-making capacity is the MacArthur Competence Assessment Tool, which is based on the aforementioned four cognitive criteria. However, not all authors agree that expressing a choice, understanding, appreciation, and reasoning are necessary and sufficient conditions for the possession of decision-making capacity (Charland 1998; White 1994; Tan et al. 2006; Breden and Vollmann 2004; Halpern and Arnold 2008; Hermann et al. 2016).

I contend that agency and decision-making capacity do not coincide. In my view, the cognitive abilities at the basis of the notion of decision-making capacity used in medical contexts are fundamental but not sufficient for the exercise of agency. I do not deal with the empirical standards, studies, and tests for assessing the presence of agency in patients, as this topic would lead my analysis too far astray and would require investigating the effects on agency of each medical condition affecting one's decision-making. However, my minimal, realistic model of the agent provides a fundamental theoretical basis for verifying the presence of agency in a patient: whether the patient has a set of normative principles of actions that she wants to pursue and that she expresses in words or behavior. When the patient has such a set of principles, she has a fundamental form of agency and can be considered an agent.

Jaworska (1999, 2007, 2017b) proposes a capacity that can signal whether one has a set of normative principles and thus a fundamental form of agency. Jaworska (1999) contends that patients in the middle stage of dementia, who are usually deemed incompetent according to the cognitive criteria for decision-making capacity, still retain the *capacity to care* or *value*. Caring is a special form of motivation (Jaworska 2007, 480) that involves a structure of emotions depending on the object of care—for instance, joy when the object is fine, frustration in response to its misfortunes, and grief at its loss. The agent attributes importance to her object of care (not necessarily consciously), which can be considered a value of the agent (Jaworska 2007, 483–84). The capacity to care is the necessary and sufficient condition of *full moral standing* and the basis of autonomy, according to Jaworska (1999, 130). Full moral standing is the moral status attributed to persons and consists of the possession of interests that matter more than those of other beings and that matter equally in moral decisions in which the interests of other beings with full moral standing are involved (Jaworska 2007,

460–61). If one sacrifices these interests in making a decision, she incurs a moral cost. For this reason, in Jaworska's view, if the patient retains the capacity to care, her current interests have full moral authority and, if they conflict with her earlier instructions regarding future medical treatments, the latter should not be enforced because they do not express the patient's current interests. In this view, the capacity to care distinguishes a patient in the early and mild stages of dementia from one in the late stage of dementia, for the former retains the capacity to care and the latter has lost it (Jaworska 1999, 123, 134–35). The normative principles of action of my minimal, realistic model of the agent can be considered the objects of care (i.e., the values) of Jaworska's approach. Jaworska affirms that a patient who loses the capacity to enact her values but retains them can be aided by caregivers and healthcare personnel in translating them into activities in the world (Jaworska 1999, 126), whereas a patient who loses the capacity to value cannot be aided in valuing things (Jaworska 1999, 122–23). In fact, lacking values means lacking the very basis for making a decision: the reasons for actions. This is why Jaworska considers the capacity to care as the basis of one's autonomy, although she adds that full-blown autonomy also requires the four components of decision-making capacity (Jaworska 1999, 130). Similarly, I contend that if the patient possesses a set of normative principles but has some impairments in decision-making capacity, she is an agent that can be helped to pursue them—in other words, supported in her agency.

4. The personal identity problem in the bioethical debate on the validity of advance directives

In the bioethical debate on advance directives, the classic conflict between the current interests of a patient and her previous interests expressed in her advance directive is the case of Margo (Firlik 1991). Margo was a patient with Alzheimer's disease first described by Andrew Firlik, a medical student who visited her for a gerontology elective. Firlik describes Margo as one of the happiest people he had known, who retained some hobbies (e.g., listening to music, painting, reading mysteries) and was happy to see him every day, even though she did not remember his name. Margo did not sign any advance directives. To analyze the conflict between an individual's precedent and current will, Dworkin imagines that, before the onset of the disease, Margo had signed a document directing that, in the event that she developed Alzheimer's disease, she should not receive medical treatment for any life-threatening disease she might develop (Dworkin 1993, 226).[5]

Three viewpoints can be outlined in the bioethical debate on advance directives in the case of dementia. One position contends that, in the event of conflict between the patient's current and former wills, the former will

100 The Moral Theory of Prudence in practice

that is laid down in advance directives remains in force, as the patient with dementia has lost the capacity for autonomy (Dworkin 1993, 1986). The opposing view affirms that the patient's current will is overriding and thus advance directives lose their authority when the patient has a good quality of life (Dresser and Robertson 1989). More recently, Jaworska has defended the thesis that, as the capacity to care is the foundation of autonomy and patients manifest this capacity until the middle stage of dementia, they are autonomous and thus their will must be respected as long as they have such a capacity (Jaworska 1999, 2007).

I focus my analysis of the bioethical debate on advance directives on one argument—the *personal identity problem*—for two reasons. First, my minimal, realistic model of the agent enables me to consider such a problem from an alternative perspective and, second, the Moral Theory of Prudence provides a new approach with which to analyze such a problem and assess the validity of advance directives. I do not discuss their moral authority on the basis of other arguments.

4.1 The personal identity problem in advance directives

Buchanan defines the personal identity problem as a "profound and potentially grave threat to the moral authority of advance directives" (Buchanan 1988, cit., 280). The personal identity problem is an objection to the moral authority of advance directives put forth by Dresser. It consists of the adoption of a personal identity view inspired by the Parfitian relation R in conjunction with the following argument: (i) one's advance directive has moral authority only over a person's life, not somebody's else life; (ii) a person with a severe neurological damage such as dementia is metaphysically distinct from the person who existed prior to the damage; (iii) therefore, if the person before the damage is numerically different from the person after the damage, the former should not dictate the medical care that the latter receives. In other words, in the case of dementia, the advance directive of the person before the disease has no moral authority on the medical treatment of the person with the disease (Dresser 1986, 1995).

Dresser endorses a psychological criterion of personal identity based on Parfit's relation R. According to Dresser, dementia could cause significant memory loss and other psychological changes to the point that the person before the disease is no longer psychologically connected with the person after the disease, namely, psychological continuity is disrupted (Dresser 1986, 1995). Dementia has also been characterized as a transformative experience (Walsh 2020).[6] As previously discussed,[7] Parfit contends that what matters in assessing whether two subjects are the same person is not the identity relation between them, and thus personal identity, but rather relation *R*. By contrast, in the personal identity problem, the criterion of identity is the continuity of a person's mental states over time, as in Locke's concept of personal identity. For Locke, a person is a thinking intelligent being that thinks of herself as persisting over time (Locke 2013 [1694], II.27.9: 335). If advance directives are justified only by one's autonomy, a weak or absent relation *R* between one's earlier and later selves undermines their moral authority, as they can only be applied to the same numerically identical person. For a defender of the personal identity problem, Margo's advance directive has no moral force and should not be applied because Margo affected by dementia is numerically different from Margo before the onset of the disease.

In sum, the personal identity problem holds that, in order to be normatively valid, advance directives require unity of personal identity over time. On the basis of the psychological criterion of identity, a patient affected by a condition causing neurological damage such as dementia can be considered a distinct person from the one who existed before that condition. Therefore, her previous advance directive lacks moral authority.

Robertson (1991) reaches a conclusion similar to Dresser's regarding advance directives, but he contends that, when a patient becomes incompetent, only a qualitative—not metaphysical—change has occurred. In such a case, the person's interests have changed radically with respect to her previous ones, but she is the same person as the one who existed prior to the onset of the disease (Robertson 1991, 7). Accordingly, Robertson contends that advance directives should not be enforced when they represent previous interests of the competent person that are in conflict with the new interests of the incompetent person (Robertson 1991, 7).

4.2 Replies to the personal identity problem in advance directives

There are three main strategies for rejecting the personal identity problem and reaffirming the moral authority of advance directives. The first strategy consists of questioning the psychological criterion of identity and refuting premise (ii) (i.e., the person with a severe neurological damage is metaphysically distinct from the person before the damage). Defenders of the narrative view of personal identity argue that persons are basically their stories. The narrative criterion of personal identity is a person's self-conception in a narrative form, namely how one thinks of oneself in terms of a narrative, thus as a persisting subject over time (Rich 1997; Blustein 1999; Kuczewski 1994, 1999; Schechtman 1996; Dworkin 1986, 1993, ch. 8; Brody 2003).

Kuczewski holds that one's identity is part of a group formed by other people that transcends one's individual consciousness and psychological continuity (Kuczewski 1994, 42). According to Kuczewski, a person's story has a prima facie moral requirement to be completed in a manner consistent with one's values in life and the normative force of advance directives derives from this moral requirement (Kuczewski 1999, 33).

Dworkin analyzes the possible conflict between a person's past interests and her current interests as an incompetent patient with dementia on the basis of one assumption: "the competent and demented selves are parts of the *same* person" (Dworkin 1986, cit., 5, italics in original). For Dworkin, personal identity survives until the last stage of dementia. He grounds one's right to autonomy on the *integrity view*, which is a narrative notion of the person: persons shape their lives according to their distinctive and consistent interests, characters, and beliefs (Dworkin 1986, 8). Whether a patient has the right to autonomy depends on whether she possesses the capacity for integrity, which is the capacity to direct her life according to a consistent scheme of values (Dworkin 1986, 10). In the integrity view, advance directives have a moral authority that is based on a person's right to autonomy. Such an authority overrides the possible conflicting interests of the patient who has lost the capacity for integrity and thus autonomy (Dworkin 1986, 13). In this framework, the person's decision about her future treatments is a decision about the shape of life that that she wants to lead if she became incompetent (Dworkin 1986, 11).

Newton and DeGrazia present other two views of personal identity that reject the personal identity problem by refuting the psychological criterion of identity. Newton contends that personal identity is founded in one's bodily continuity; thus, disruption of psychological continuity does not threaten a patient's identity with herself before the disease (Newton 1999, 195). DeGrazia affirms that humans are essentially animals, not persons. As one's animality survives one's loss of psychological continuity, the patient is not metaphysically distinct from herself before the disease (DeGrazia 1999, 383).

The second strategy for rejecting the personal identity problem questions the conclusion (iii) of its argument. This strategy contends that the fact that the person before the disease is numerically different from the person after the disease does not undermine the moral authority of advance directives. Buchanan and Brock (1989), Kuhse (1999), and Persad (2019) accept the Lockean view of personal identity (Persad, Buchanan, and Brock accept it only for the sake of the argument) and contend that one's identity over time is not necessary for the validity of advance directives.

Buchanan and Brock (Buchanan 1988; Buchanan and Brock 1989, ch. 3) hold that the patient in the late stage of dementia has lost her personhood. The fact that she is not a person does not equate to the loss of moral status (Buchanan 1988, 284; Buchanan and Brock 1989, 160), but it means that the interests of the person before the disease have greater moral worth than

The Moral Theory of Prudence in practice 103

the interests of the individual in the late stage of dementia. Among a person's interests, Buchanan and Brock identify a type called *surviving interests*: those surviving the person to which they belong, such as the interest in the treatment of one's corpse. Their satisfaction depends on events that happen after the person has ceased to exist (Buchanan 1988, 287; Buchanan and Brock 1989, 164). For these authors, advance directives express a person's surviving interests about the medical treatment of her "living remains" (Buchanan 1988, cit., 287), namely the person's successor without personhood. Furthermore, they contend that, as long as the psychological continuity between the author of the advance directive and the subject of such a directive reaches a threshold necessary for the persistence of personal identity, advance directives have full moral authority. In cases that fall below the threshold, the moral authority of advance directives diminishes with the diminishing of psychological continuity (Buchanan 1988, 297; Buchanan and Brock 1989, 183–84).

Kuhse (1999) agrees with Buchanan and Brock that the patient in the late stage of dementia has lost personhood, but, unlike them, she states that only personhood has intrinsic value and that the interests of the patient are not morally worthy once the latter has lost personhood (Kuhse 1999, 359–60). Kuhse founds the moral authority of advance directives on the difference in moral worth between the patient's interests and those that she used to have when she was a person. According to Kuhse, a person's previous interest in the refusal of life-sustaining treatment stated in advance directives should be honored in the case that the subject of such an advance directive loses personhood. This is because, according to Kuhse, a person is a being who is interested in continuing to live. When someone lacks this interest because she has lost personhood, she is not harmed by being allowed to die painlessly (e.g., by not giving her life-sustaining care), and letting her die painlessly is thus not morally wrong (Kuhse 1999, 359–60).

Persad (2019) proposes that advance directives are based on the person's right of property to the body that has survived her and is affected by dementia. Persad stated that a person's right over her body has been acquired by historical embodiment (i.e., by being the first one to be embodied in that body) and lasts even after the right holder has ceased to exist (Persad 2019, 249–50).

The final strategy for rejecting the personal identity problem consists of showing the negative effects on society of adopting the psychological criterion of identity. For Rhoden, accepting such a criterion would subvert the institutions on which society is built, as it would undermine, for instance, the criminal justice system, the duty to honor one's contracts, and, in general, responsibility for past deeds (Rhoden 1990, 854). Rich contends that adopting the psychological criterion of identity would legitimate the distribution of the legacy of a person with dementia before she is declared dead (Rich 1997, 146).

5. An alternative perspective on the personal identity problem: The practical level of the agent

According to the personal identity problem, advance directives are interpersonal decisions, as the person who exists after a neurological damage is considered different from the one who existed prior to the damage. On the contrary, if the two are considered the same metaphysical entity, advance directives are intrapersonal decisions.

As seen in Chapter 2, I interpret diachronic self-regarding decisions as interagential, namely as conflicts between a person's later and earlier selves. This interpretation does not entail that the two selves are two distinct entities from the person to which they belong from a metaphysical perspective.[8] In Chapter 2, I contended that what is relevant for the analysis of a self-regarding decision is the significant entity of the practical sphere, namely the agent.[9] This is because agents necessitate only a practical concept of themselves to be effective in the sphere of action. In the following analysis, one's present self is the earlier self drawing her advance directive, while one's future self is the later self to whom the advance directive pertains (i.e., the self who will be subject to the decisions expressed in the advance directive).

The minimal, realistic model of the agent enables the refutation of the personal identity problem of advance directives by shifting the discussion from the metaphysical level of personal identity to the practical level of the agent. In the minimal, realistic model of the agent, one's diachronic selves involved in an advance directive are two practical entities situated at different temporal stages of the metaphysical entity (i.e., the person) of whom they are part; each self coexists with the person.

The personal identity problem states that advance directives are valid only if, first, the individual subject to such directives is numerically identical to the author of the advance directive and, second, the criterion of identity between the two is psychological. I argue that adjudicating the validity of advance directives does not depend on the metaphysical question of the criterion of personal identity—that is, whether personal identity resides in psychological (Dresser 1986, 1995), bodily (Newton 1999), or narrative continuity (Rich 1997; Blustein 1999; Kuczewski 1994, 1999; Schechtman 1996; Dworkin 1986, 1993, ch. 8; Brody 2003). Nor does the validity of advance directives depend on whether personal identity is irrelevant and rather relation R (Parfit 1984) or humans' animality (DeGrazia 1999) is the only criterion that counts in adjudicating whether two individuals are the same. Like Robertson (1991), I read the changes in one's later self affected by a medical condition as a person's qualitative changes that do not give rise to a numerically different metaphysical entity. Such changes regard the diachronic selves, namely the practical level of the agents. If a person's later self has different core normative principles of action, then she is a numerically different agent from the person's earlier self, but her substratum—the metaphysical person of whom she is a part—is the same as that of the earlier self. Unlike Robertson, however, I do not conclude that advance directives are not valid if they conflict with the changed interests of the patient. In the next section, I assess the validity of advance directives on the basis of whether the patient is an agent.

In addition, I contend that, without delving into the issue of personal identity, the individuals before and after the disease have something that guarantees a connection between them within the framework of the minimal, realistic model of the agent. Such a connection is the strong causal relation between one's earlier and later selves, which is the fourth feature of the present-self–future-self relationship:[10] the earlier self's mental states affect each following mental state and thus the later self's mental states.

Gligorov and Vitrano (2011) hold that the assessment of the validity of advance directives does not involve the metaphysical level of personal identity but rather a practical concept of psychological continuity (Gligorov and Vitrano 2011, 151). They turned psychological continuity as a criterion of metaphysical identity into *psychological similarity* as a practical criterion for the assessment of the normative authority of advance directives. Psychological similarity describes the sharing of memories, goals, beliefs, and intentions between two of an individual's time slices or selves (Gligorov and Vitrano 2011, 152). Gligorov and Vitrano's psychological similarity is a criterion of qualitative change. In other words, they maintain that, in cases of significant psychological shifts due to illness, the metaphysical entity before and after the illness are the same entity, even though the individual after the illness may undergo radical psychological changes that disrupt her psychological continuity—and thus psychological similarity—with the author of the advance directive (Gligorov and Vitrano 2011, 157). Gligorov and Vitrano indicate that psychological similarity is maintained as long as one's core values and preferences about one's treatment remain the same across time (Gligorov and Vitrano 2011, 157). They conclude that advance directives are valid and should thus be enforced when there is sufficient psychological similarity between the author of the advance directive and the individual subject to those directives.

The perspective from which I analyze the personal identity problem in advance directives is similar to that of Gligorov and Vitrano: we both avoid metaphysical claims about the continuity of a person and deal instead with the practical level of advance directives. However, Gligorov and Vitrano look for a relationship or connection between two selves at the practical level (i.e., psychological similarity) without providing a model or definition of such selves from the practical perspective and propose assessing the validity of advance directives on the basis of that relationship of similarity. In contrast, I analyze the validity of advance directives on the basis of an account of one's diachronic selves as practical agents whose relationship with one another is regulated by moral principles. What the latter says about advance directives is the subject of the next section.

6. Application of the Moral Theory of Prudence to advance directives in the case of dementia

In the debate on the personal identity problem, the Moral Theory of Prudence enables the shift of the assessment criterion of the validity of advance directives from the issue of personal identity to the presence of agency. I contend that, in order to answer the question: "Do advance directives have moral authority in the case of significant psychological changes?", we first need to ask: "Is the individual subject to the advance directive still an agent or at least presumed as such?" For the sake of simplicity, I assume that someone either is or is not an agent, I do not consider gray areas. As contended in section 3.2, the fundamental element for verifying the presence of agency in a patient is whether the patient has a set of normative principles of actions that she wants to pursue and that she expresses in words or behavior. I call the patient with advance directive whose possession of agency is under examination as the *later individual* of a person.

Advance directives are a strategy for partly limiting the objective ignorance of a person's earlier self with regard to the later self because they contain one's instructions about medical care in various circumstances and in the event that a certain medical condition occurs. However, because of the indeterminacy of the later self (the second feature of the present-self–future-self relationship),[11] it is not possible to forecast what the later self will want and whether she will refute what the earlier self decides in the advance directive. In addition, the earlier self does not know some relevant future events, such as advances in medical treatments. The later self may miss out on such advances if the earlier self's advance directive requires medical providers to cease or not provide some treatment in the future.

In both the cases in which one's later individual is an agent and those in which she is not, it can be assessed whether a person's earlier self who is writing the advance directive has forward-looking self-regarding responsibility for such directives to her later individual. If a person's earlier self satisfies the three conditions for the attribution of forward-looking self-regarding responsibility, she has such a responsibility. These three conditions are having causal control over the outcome of one's actions, being able to consider the predictable effects of one's actions, and choosing without any coercion.[12]

In the event that a person signed an advance directive and her later individual is an agent or presumed as such, the latter is in a vulnerable position. In fact, because of the asymmetry of decisional power between one's earlier and later selves (the first feature of the present-self–future-self relationship),[13] the earlier self decides which medical treatment the individual's later self will undergo, and the later self cannot take part in the decision. In advance directives, the potential conflict between one's earlier and later selves is not problematic as long as the later self is assessed as competent, as she can revoke or modify the previous directives, if she has different ideas about her medical treatments. Advance directives are problematic when the later individual is assessed as incompetent but is still an agent because I contended that agency and decision-making capacity as defined in the medical context do not coincide. As long as the patient is an agent, she has the same moral status and thus the same rights that she had before the medical condition.

The Moral Theory of Prudence establishes that one's earlier self has the obligation to preserve the future self's agency and that the latter has the right to an open present.[14] Therefore, the theory requires that, as long as the later individual is an agent or presumed as such, advance directives undermining the necessary conditions for the pursuit of her normative principles are not morally valid and thus cannot be enforced. Whether the earlier and later selves have the same core normative principles—and thus are numerically identical—is not relevant for assessing the validity of advance directives on the basis of the Moral Theory of Prudence. What is relevant is rather the presence of agency in the later self; if agency is present, only advance directives preserving the later self's agency are morally legitimate from the perspective of the Moral Theory of Prudence.

Let us consider Margo's case through the framework of the Moral Theory of Prudence. When young and healthy, Margo decides that, if she is affected by dementia in the future and develops an infection, she does not want to be treated with antibiotics. This will most likely result in letting herself die in the event that she contracts an infection. Letting oneself die is a violation of the right to an open present, as it nullifies the future self's pursuit of her set of normative principles. If, in someone's life, there are no other reasons for letting oneself die that are weightier than the right to an open present (e.g., ceasing the present self's suffering due to a chronic painful state), the Moral Theory of Prudence prohibits letting oneself die.[15] The theory demands that as long as Margo affected by dementia is an agent and has no overriding reasons to let herself die, the young and healthy Margo's advance directive should not be enforced.

If the individual subject to an advance directive is not an agent, the Moral Theory of Prudence does not apply since such a case is not a diachronic self-regarding decision. In this case, advance directives violating the open present of a person's later individual are not illegitimate because there is no open present to protect, since this later individual is not an agent. However, the fact that a later individual is not an agent does not imply that she has no moral status; rather, it indicates that she does not have the same moral status as the agent. As Quante (1999) observed, an incompetent patient who can feel pain "cannot simply be treated like an ethically neutral object" (Quante 1999, cit., 372); rather, according to him, the incompetent patient's interests should be weighed against the advance directive that she previously signed (Quante 1999, 372). I contend that an agent has a higher moral status than a later individual who does not have agency. Hence, if the interests of a person's earlier self conflict with the interests of this person's later individual, the former are morally weightier than the latter.

The studies presented in Chapter 1 regarding people's perceptions of their future selves as distinct individuals on whom people are willing to impose burdens add another element to the bioethical discussion of advance directives (Ersner-Hershfield et al. 2009a, 2009b; Hershfield et al. 2011; Pronin et al. 2008; Mitchell et al. 2011; Bartels and Urminsky 2011, 2015; Pronin and Ross 2006). Autonomy is the foundation of the authority of advance directives, but it should not be interpreted in terms of the capacity to be the best judge of one's present and future interests. In fact, these studies showed that individuals tend to favor their present selves over their future selves, which is a tendency that has long-term negative effects on their future selves.[16]

After having examined the requirements of the Moral Theory of Prudence in advance directives at the theoretical level, I can sketch a possible implementation of that theory in advance directives. As I have contended that agency does not coincide with decision-making capacity, there can be cases in which the patient is still an agent but is deemed incompetent, thus losing the ability to amend her advance directive. Hence, advance directives should include the clause that as long as the patient expresses her normative principles in words or behavior and thus can be presumed an agent, advance directives violating the patient's open present are not applicable unless moral reasons weightier than the right to an open present are at stake. This strategy limits the vulnerability of a person's later self and enables the respect of this later self's open present. In addition, one could be supported in writing her advance directive by making her aware of her bias toward her present self. This could increase the individual's concern for the later self and render her a better judge of her interests (Viganò 2018).

7. Conclusion

Advance directives are decisions made by one's earlier self that have significant effects on one's later self to the point that the decision made by the present self can completely close the later self's open present by letting the latter die. Advance directives are a fundamental means of exercising one's own autonomy in healthcare, but in the case of dementia, they can be a hindrance to the patient's autonomy, if she is an agent but deemed incompetent. The Moral Theory of Prudence enables the protection of such a patient.

On the basis of the minimal, realistic account of the agent, I rejected the personal identity problem in advance directives by contending that the personal identity issue is not relevant to adjudicating the validity of advance directives and that the latter pertains to two diachronic selves who are part of the same person. It is true that the patient with dementia undertakes psychological shifts, but my thesis is that such changes are qualitative (i.e., occurring to the same person) and not metaphysical (i.e., giving rise to a numerically different entity).

When employed in the debate surrounding the personal identity problem, the Moral Theory of Prudence enables the assessment of the validity of advance directives on the basis of the presence of agency. As a consequence, I contended that, in this debate, the relevant question is not: "Is the individual after the psychological shift the same metaphysical entity as before?" but: "Is the individual after the psychological shift still an agent?"

I argued that, as long as one is an agent or presumed as such, advance directives can be read as diachronic self-regarding decisions. If the patient is still an agent, the Moral Theory of Prudence holds that she has the right to an open present. This means that advance directives violating an agent's open present are not valid unless there are weightier reasons at hand, such as ceasing the suffering caused by a condition of chronic pain. Moreover, the Moral Theory of Prudence holds that the earlier self has the obligation to preserve the later self's agency when making decisions about future medical treatments. If the patient is not an agent, I contended that advance directives violating the patient's open present are not illegitimate because there is no open present that can be undermined, as there is no longer any agent. When applied to advance directives in dementia, the Moral Theory of Prudence helps protect the patient's agency. If agency is no longer present, the theory demands that caregivers and healthcare professionals respect the patient's previous agency, which is expressed in her advance directive.

Notes

1. In my analysis, I do not consider the present and future selves of the Russian nobleman's wife because her present and future selves are involved in a diachronic moral conflict that is not self-regarding: the wife's conflicting moral requirements (i.e., keeping a promise to her young husband versus revoking it as required by the old husband) derive from the Russian nobleman, not from her later and earlier selves.
2. See Chapter 2, section 3.2.
3. See Chapter 2, section 3.2.
4. See Chapter 2, section 4.
5. Jaworska (1999, 135) observes that although Dworkin contends that he wants to deal with the late stage of dementia, Margo's case is not representative of such a stage; Margo is rather in the middle stage. This observation is relevant because, in the late stage of dementia, there are no conflicts between a person's earlier and current interests, since patients are usually unresponsive and do not express their interests in words or behavior.
6. More precisely, Walsh describes dementia as a *cognitive* transformative experience, namely an experience that "alters a person's cognitive capacities in such a way that may change the way the person thinks about their preferences, values, and beliefs" (Walsh 2020, cit., 58).
7. See Chapter 2, section 2.2.
8. See Chapter 2, section 3.1, and Chapter 3, section 3.2.
9. See Chapter 2, section 3.1.
10. See Chapter 2, section 4.
11. See Chapter 2, section 4.
12. See Chapter 3, section 2.3.
13. See Chapter 2, section 4.
14. See Chapter 3, sections 2.1 and 2.2.
15. As explained in Chapter 3, section 2.2, the Moral Theory of Prudence pertains one aspect of a person's practical sphere, which is her relationship with her future self in diachronic self-regarding decisions, and consists of pro tanto moral principles that can be overridden by other ones. Assessing the weight of a moral consideration that comes from another part of a person's practical sphere is beyond the scope of the Moral Theory of Prudence.
16. See Chapter 1, section 2, and Chapter 2, section 2.3.

References

American Psychiatric Association. 2013. *Diagnostic and Statistical Manual of Mental Disorders*, 5th ed. Arlington: American Psychiatric Association. https://doi.org/10.1176/appi.books.9780890425596.744053.

Bartels, Daniel M., and Oleg Urminsky. 2011. "On Intertemporal Selfishness: How the Perceived Instability of Identity Underlies Impatient Consumption." *Journal of Consumer Research* 38 (1): 182–98. https://doi.org/10.1086/658339.

———. 2015. "To Know and to Care: How Awareness and Valuation of the Future Jointly Shape Consumer Spending." *Journal of Consumer Research* 41 (6): 1469–85. https://doi.org/10.1086/680670.

Blustein, Jeffrey. 1999. "Choosing for Others as Continuing a Life Story: The Problem of Personal Identity Revisited." *Journal of Law, Medicine and Ethics* 27 (1): 20–31. https://doi.org/10.1111/j.1748-720X.1999.tb01432.x.
Breden, Torsten Marcus, and Jochen Vollmann. 2004. "The Cognitive Based Approach of Capacity Assessment in Psychiatry: A Philosophical Critique of the MacCAT-T." *Health Care Analysis*. https://doi.org/10.1007/s10728-004-6635-x.
Brody, Howard. 2003. *Stories of Sickness*. New York: Oxford University Press.
Buchanan, Allen E. 1988. "Advance Directives and the Personal Identity Problem." *Philosophy and Public Affairs* 17 (4): 277–302.
Buchanan, Allen E., and Dan W. Brock. 1989. *Deciding for Others: The Ethics of Surrogate Decision Making*. Cambridge: Cambridge University Press. https://doi.org/10.1017/s0829320100002957.
Charland, Louis C. 1998. "Is Mr. Spock Mentally Competent? Competence to Consent and Emotion." *Philosophy, Psychiatry, & Psychology* 5 (1): 67–81.
DeGrazia, David. 1999. "Advance Directives, Dementia, and 'the Someone Else Problem.'" *Bioethics* 13 (5): 373–91. https://doi.org/10.1111/1467-8519.00166.
Dresser, Rebecca S. 1986. "Life, Death, and Incompetent Patients: Conceptual Infirmities and Hidden Values in the Law." *Arizona Law Review* 28 (3): 373–405.
———. 1995. "Dworkin on Dementia: Elegant Theory, Questionable Policy." *Hastings Center Report* 25 (6): 32–38. https://doi.org/10.2307/3527839.
Dresser, Rebecca S., and John A. Robertson. 1989. "Quality of Life and Non-Treatment Decisions for Incompetent Patients: A Critique of the Orthodox Approach." *The Journal of Law, Medicine & Ethics* 17 (3): 234–44. https://doi.org/10.1111/j.1748-720X.1989.tb01101.x.
Dworkin, Ronald. 1986. "Autonomy and the Demented Self." *The Milbank Quarterly* 64: 4–16. https://doi.org/10.2307/3349959.
———. 1993. *Life's Dominion: An Argument About Abortion, Euthanasia, and Individual Freedom*. New York: Alfred A. Knopf, Inc. https://doi.org/10.1525/sp.2007.54.1.23.
Ersner-Hershfield, Hal, M. Tess Garton, Kacey Ballard, Gregory R. Samanez-Larkin, and Brian Knutson. 2009a. "Don't Stop Thinking About Tomorrow: Individual Differences in Future Self-Continuity Account for Saving." *Judgment and Decision Making* 4 (4): 280–86.
Ersner-Hershfield, Hal, G. Elliott Wimmer, and Brian Knutson. 2009b. "Saving for the Future Self: Neural Measures of Future Self-Continuity Predict Temporal Discounting." *Social Cognitive and Affective Neuroscience* 4 (1): 85–92. https://doi.org/10.1093/scan/nsn042.
Firlik, Andrew D. 1991. "Margo's Logo." *Journal of the American Medical Association* 265 (2): 201. https://doi.org/10.1001/jama.1991.03460020055013.
Gligorov, Nada, and Christine Vitrano. 2011. "The Impact of Personal Identity on Advance Directives." *Journal of Value Inquiry* 45 (2): 147–58. https://doi.org/10.1007/s10790-011-9277-x.
Grisso, Thomas, and Paul S. Appelbaum. 1998. *Assessing Competence to Consent to Treatment: A Guide for Physicians and Other Health Professionals*. New York and London: Oxford University Press.

Halpern, Jodi, and Robert M. Arnold. 2008. "Affective Forecasting: An Unrecognized Challenge in Making Serious Health Decisions." *Journal of General Internal Medicine*. https://doi.org/10.1007/s11606-008-0719-5.

Hermann, Helena, Manuel Trachsel, Bernice S. Elger, and Nikola Biller-Andorno. 2016. "Emotion and Value in the Evaluation of Medical Decision-Making Capacity: A Narrative Review of Arguments." *Frontiers in Psychology* 7 (765): 1–10. https://doi.org/10.3389/fpsyg.2016.00765.

Hershfield, Hal E., Daniel G. Goldstein, William F. Sharpe, Jesse Fox, Leo Yeykelis, Laura L. Carstensen, and Jeremy N. Bailenson. 2011. "Increasing Saving Behavior Through Age-Progressed Renderings of the Future Self." *Journal of Marketing Research* 48: S23–S37. https://doi.org/10.1509/jmkr.48.SPL.S23.

Jaworska, A. 1999. "Respecting the Margins of Agency: Alzheimer's Patients and the Capacity to Value." *Philosophy & Public Affairs* 28 (2): 105–38. https://doi.org/10.1111/j.1088-4963.1999.00105.x.

———. 2007. "Caring and Full Moral Standing." *Ethics* 117 (3): 460–97. https://doi.org/10.1086/512780.

———. 2017a. "Advance Directives and Substitute Decision-Making." In *Stanford Encyclopedia of Philosophy*, edited by E. N. Zalta. Accessed July 31, 2021. https://plato.stanford.edu/entries/advance-directives/

———. 2017b. "Ethical Dilemmas in Neurodegenerative Disease: Respecting Patients at the Twilight of Agency." In *Neuroethics: Anticipating the Future*, edited by J. Illes. Oxford: Oxford University Press.

Kuczewski, Mark G. 1994. "Whose Will Is It, Anyway? A Discussion of Advance Directives, Personal Identity, and Consensus in Medical Ethics." *Bioethics* 8 (1): 27–48. https://doi.org/10.1111/j.1467-8519.1994.tb00240.x.

———. 1999. "Commentary: Narrative Views of Personal Identity and Substituted Judgment in Surrogate Decision Making." *The Journal of Law, Medicine & Ethics* 27 (1): 32–36. https://doi.org/10.1111/j.1748-720X.1999.tb01433.x.

Kuhse, Helga. 1999. "Some Reflections on the Problem of Advance Directives, Personhood, and Personal Identity." *Kennedy Institute of Ethics Journal* 9 (4): 347–64. https://doi.org/10.1353/ken.1999.0027.

Locke, John. 2013 [1694]. *An Essay Concerning Human Understanding*. Edited by P. H. Nidditch. Oxford: Oxford University Press.

Mitchell, Jason P., Jessica Schirmer, Daniel L. Ames, and Daniel T. Gilbert. 2011. "Medial Prefrontal Cortex Predicts Intertemporal Choice." *Journal of Cognitive Neuroscience* 23 (4): 857–66. https://doi.org/10.1162/jocn.2010.21479.

Newton, Michael J. 1999. "Precedent Autonomy: Life-Sustaining Intervention and the Demented Patient." *Cambridge Quarterly of Healthcare Ethics* 8 (2): 189–99. https://doi.org/10.1017/S0963180199802084.

Parfit, Derek. 1984. *Reasons and Persons*. Oxford: Clarendon Press.

Persad, Govind. 2019. "Authority Without Identity: Defending Advance Directives via Posthumous Rights Over One's Body." *Journal of Medical Ethics* 45 (4): 249–56. https://doi.org/10.1136/medethics-2018-104971.

Pronin, Emily, Christopher Y. Olivola, and Kathleen A. Kennedy. 2008. "Doing Unto Future Selves As You Would Do Unto Others: Psychological Distance and

Decision Making." *Personality and Social Psychology Bulletin* 34 (2): 224–36. https://doi.org/10.1177/0146167207310023.

Pronin, Emily, and Lee Ross. 2006. "Temporal Differences in Trait Self-Ascription: When the Self Is Seen as an Other." *Journal of Personality and Social Psychology* 90 (2): 197–209. https://doi.org/10.1037/0022-3514.90.2.197.

Quante, Michael. 1999. "Precedent Autonomy and Personal Identity." *Kennedy Institute of Ethics Journal* 9 (4): 365–81. https://doi.org/10.1353/ken.1999.0028.

Rhoden, Nancy K. 1990. "The Limits of Legal Objectivity." *North Carolina Law Review* 68 (5): 845–65.

Rich, Ben A. 1997. "Prospective Autonomy and Critical Interests: A Narrative Defense of the Moral Authority of Advance Directives." *Cambridge Quarterly of Healthcare Ethics* 6 (2): 138–47. https://doi.org/10.1017/s0963180100007763.

Robertson, John A. 1991. "Second Thoughts on Living Wills." *The Hastings Center Report* 21 (6): 6. https://doi.org/10.2307/3562355.

Schechtman, Marya. 1996. *The Constitution of Selves*. Ithaca: Cornell University Press.

Tan, Jacinta A., Tony Hope, Anne Stewart, and Raymond Fitzpatrick. 2006. "Competence to Make Treatment Decisions in Anorexia Nervosa: Thinking Processes and Values." *Philosophy, Psychiatry, & Psychology* 13 (4): 267–82. https://doi.org/10.1353/ppp.2007.0032.

Trachsel, Manuel, Helena Hermann, and Nikola Biller-Andorno. 2015. "Cognitive Fluctuations as a Challenge for the Assessment of Decision-Making Capacity in Patients With Dementia." *American Journal of Alzheimer's Disease and Other Dementias* 30 (4): 360–63. https://doi.org/10.1177/1533317514539377.

Viganò, Eleonora. 2018. "The Individual's Later Self Is Less Autonomous and a Stranger: The Impact of Time in Advance Directives." *Bioethica Forum* 11 (4): 165–67.

Walsh, Emily. 2020. "Cognitive Transformation, Dementia, and the Moral Weight of Advance Directives." *American Journal of Bioethics* 20 (8): 54–64. https://doi.org/10.1080/15265161.2020.1781955.

White, Becky Cox. 1994. *Competence to Consent*. Washington: Georgetown University Press.

Conclusion

Doing the right thing for other people is only a part of morality, not the whole story. We also stand in a relationship with ourselves that needs to be investigated at the empirical level and regulated by a normative moral theory. Our relationships with ourselves belong to the realm of prudence, namely, care for oneself that aims to one's well-being.

In this book, I attempted to provide a better understanding of the relationship in which we stand with our future selves in diachronic self-regarding decisions. To this end, I elaborated two theories. The first is the overarching IC theory of the perceived future self, which is an empirical theory of prudential perception that connects and integrates the IC theories about our perceptions of our future selves. The overarching IC theory of the perceived future self is based on three principles: (1) the individual's mental simulation of her future selves increases her perceived continuity with her future self; (2) the individual's low psychological continuity with her future self decreases the likelihood that she mentally simulates her future self; and (3) the individual mentally represents the future self at various degrees of abstractedness, which are influenced by her perceived continuity with her future self.

The second theory I elaborated is the Moral Theory of Prudence in diachronic self-regarding decisions, which regulates the relationship between one's present and future selves in such decisions. The Moral Theory of Prudence consists of three principles: (1) the obligation to preserve one's future agency, which protects the necessary conditions for the pursuit of any set of normative principles of actions; (2) the right to an open present, which consists of the future self's claim to pursue her set of normative principles of action; and (3) forward-looking self-regarding responsibility, which is the present self's responsibility to the future self for the predictable effects of the present self's actions on the future self.

The aims of this book were to clarify why we sometimes feel that, in the past, we made the wrong decision for ourselves and to provide guidance in

Conclusion 115

making the right choice for ourselves the next time. I showed that when we perceive our future selves as distinct from ourselves, we usually care less for our future selves and assign more burdens to our future selves than to our present selves. Such behavior may bring about disadvantaged conditions for our later selves in the long run and thus the doubt that our past selves (who once were present selves) made the wrong choice for our current selves (who once were future selves). The Moral Theory of Prudence helps us to make the right choice for our future selves, as it protects the latter from our earlier selves' greater decisional power and guides our present selves in making diachronic self-regarding decisions that respect our future selves' agency.

In this book, I introduced four innovative elements to the ethical reflection on diachronic self-regarding decisions that may be considered the substantial lessons and takeaways of the book. First, contrary to the mainstream view on prudence, I argued that the latter is a moral requirement for three reasons. The first is that imprudent acts inflict harm to one's future self that is not morally justified. The second is that the definition of a moral agent implies a basic form of care for oneself: the moral agent's justification of her actions to herself. The third is that, in the framework of the Moral Theory of Prudence, prudence as care for oneself entails the protection of one's agency, whose possession is a necessary condition for being moral (i.e., for moral agency).

The second innovative element of this book is the minimal, realistic model of the agent (i.e., the subject facing a diachronic self-regarding decision) on which the Moral Theory of Prudence is founded. I differentiated the person as a metaphysical substance from the self or agent as a practical entity that acts in the practical sphere. Accordingly, I conceived the relationship among a person's diachronic selves (i.e., a person's earlier and later selves) as a relationship among agents. The agent of the minimal, realistic model is a morally relevant attribute of a person endowed with a set of normative principles of actions that are her reasons for action, a minimal temporal extension, and care for the person's future self that depends on the psychological connection with her future self. This last characteristic of the agent in the minimal, realistic model makes such an agent close to Parfit's characterization of the person (Parfit 1984), which is, in turn, similar to Hume's concept of the subject as a bundle of experiences, thoughts, and actions (Hume 1928 [1738–1740]). However, the agent of the minimal realistic model is a practical and not metaphysical entity, like Korsgaard's unified agent (Korsgaard 1989, 1996). The minimal, realistic model of the agent is an empirically plausible model that avoids the excessive idealization of the agent present in the models of many approaches to diachronic self-regarding decisions. These approaches tend to assume epistemic conditions that a real agent does not fulfill and/or cognitive capacities that she does not have (Cureton 2016; Brink 2003; McKerlie 2007; Pettigrew 2020; Dorsey 2021).

The third innovative element of this book is the reading of diachronic self-regarding decisions as interagential decisions between one's present and future selves belonging to intergenerational ethics. The rationale for this interpretation is that most of the moral features of the present-self–future-self relationship are shared by the moral features of the relationship between present and future generations: the asymmetry of decisional power; the indeterminacy of the future self and future people; and the objective ignorance of the identity, existence, and conditions of the future self and future people. Different from my theory, the alternative approaches to diachronic self-regarding decisions interpret diachronic self-regarding decisions as intrapersonal (Cureton 2016; Bruckner 2003, 2004; Arvan 2020; Brink 2003; McKerlie 2007; Dorsey 2021) or interpersonal (Parfit 1984; Pettigrew 2020).

The last innovative element is the solution that I provided to diachronic self-regarding decisions: the Moral Theory of Prudence. This is as an agency-centered theory regulating the relationship among one's diachronic selves through a moral framework that is based on the respect for agency—that is, the capacity to be an agent of the diachronic selves. In contrast, several approaches to diachronic self-regarding decisions are grounded in well-being (Cureton 2016; Arvan 2020; McKerlie 2007; Pettigrew 2020). When the Moral Theory of Prudence is applied to advance healthcare directives in dementia and the connected personal identity problem, it offers a new perspective from which to adjudicate the moral authority of advance directives: their validity depends on whether the patient is still an agent. The theory holds that, if the patient subject to an advance directive is still an agent, she has the right to an open present. Therefore, advance directives undermining an agent's open present are not valid unless there are weightier reasons involved. If the patient is not an agent, the theory holds that the advance directive she previously signed cannot violate her open present because she has no open present that can be threatened by the advance directive.

Schmidtz (1997) describes eudaimonism—one of the ancient ethical theories—as entailing the realization that we are the outcomes as well as the makers of our choices, as indicated in the first quote in the epigraph of this book. Diachronic self-regarding decisions are paradigmatic in this regard. In such decisions, we have two roles: as makers, we are the subject of the choice, and, as outcomes, we are also its object. This book raises awareness of our dual roles in such decisions and enables us to navigate dexterously between the two.

References

Arvan, Marcus. 2020. *Neurofunctional Prudence and Morality*. New York: Routledge.
Brink, David O. 2003. "Prudence and Authenticity: Intrapersonal Conflicts of Value." *Philosophical Review* 112 (2): 215–45. https://doi.org/10.1215/00318108-112-2-215.
Bruckner, Donald W. 2003. "A Contractarian Account of (Part of) Prudence." *American Philosophical Quarterly* 40 (1): 33–46. https://doi.org/10.2307/20010095.
———. 2004. "Prudence and Justice." *Economics and Philosophy* 20 (1): 35–63. https://doi.org/10.1017/S0266267104001257.
Cureton, Adam. 2016. "Prudence and Responsibility to Self in an Identity Crisis." *Res Philosophica* 93 (4): 815–41. https://doi.org/10.11612/resphil.1466.
Dorsey, Dale. 2021. *A Theory of Prudence*. Oxford: Oxford University Press. https://doi.org/10.1093/oso/9780198823759.001.0001.
Hume, David. 1928 [1738–1740]. *A Treatise of Human Nature*. Edited by L. A. Selby-Bigge. Oxford: Clarendon Press.
Korsgaard, Christine M. 1989. "Personal Identity and the Unity of Agency: A Kantian Response to Parfit." *Philosophy & Public Affairs* 18 (2): 101–32.
———. 1996. *The Sources of Normativity*. New York: Cambridge University Press.
McKerlie, Dennis. 2007. "Rational Choice, Changes in Values Over Time, and Well-Being." *Utilitas* 19 (1): 51–72. https://doi.org/10.1017/S0953820806002342.
Parfit, Derek. 1984. *Reasons and Persons*. Oxford: Clarendon Press.
Pettigrew, Richard. 2020. *Choosing for Changing Selves*. Oxford: Oxford University Press.
Schmidtz, David. 1997. "Self-interest: What's in it for Me?" *Social Philosophy and Policy* 14 (1): 107–21. https://doi.org/10.1017/s0265052500001692.

Index

advance directives 94, 96–7, 99–103, 106–8
advance healthcare directives *see* advance directives
agency 3, 5, 74–5, 81, 85, 88n2, 93–4, 97–9, 106–9; future 2, 62–9; moral 45, 69
agent 46–7, 74, 76, 85, 108; idealized 76, 80, 82–3, 85, **86–7**; minimal, realistic 47–8; practical (*see* agent)
Aggregate Utility Solution 81–2, **87**
Alzheimer's disease 97, 99
Aristotle 5, 41
Arvan, M. 44, 50, 75, 77–8, 85, **86**
asymmetry of decisional power 51
authenticity 38, 67, 88n7
autonomy 41, 65–6, 96–100, 102

Brink, D. O. 78–80, **86**
Brock, D. W. 97, 102–3
Bruckner, D. 75, 77, **86**
Buchanan, A. 97, 100, 102–3
Bykvist, K. 67, 89n17

capabilities 64
capacity to care 98–100
capacity to value *see* capacity to care
care of oneself *see* prudence
care of others 2, 42, 50
Carter, I. 88n8
Categorical-Instrumental Imperative 44, 77–8, **86**
construal level theory 17–19
Cureton, A. 75–6, **86**

decisional power 51, 62–3, 66, 107, 115
decision-making capacity 5, 97–9, 107–8

decision-making competence *see* decision-making capacity
DeGrazia, D. 102
dementia 94, 96–104, 107–9
diachronic self-regarding conflicts 39, 77–82, **86–7**, 94–6
diachronic self-regarding conflicts of values *see* diachronic self-regarding conflicts
diachronic self-regarding decisions 1–3, 8, 38–40, 46, 48–50, 61–9, 75–80, 85, **86–7**
discount: social 16; temporal 3, 8–11, *21*
Dorsey, D. 83–4, **87**
Dresser, R. 100–1
duties to oneself 54n6, 72–3
Dworkin, R. 99–102

egocentricity bias 14–17, 25
emotion regulation 26, 29
emotional contagion 14, 17
empathy 11–13, 15, 17
empirical theory of prudential perception 3, 22
episodic agent 45
episodic future thinking 11–12, 25
Ersner-Hershfield, H. 24, 28n6
ethical theories: ancient 2, 41; modern 40–2
ethics: ancient (*see* ancient ethical theories); intergenerational 40, 50–2, 65, 70–1; modern (*see* modern ethical theories)

fairness 65
Feinberg, J. 65–6
full moral standing 98

future self-continuity 12, *21*; *see also* psychological continuity
future self-continuity model 12–14

Gligorov, N. 105–6
good life 2, 38, 41, 63

happiness 2, 41, 73
Hershfield, H. 12–14, 28n7
Hills, A. 89n16
hot/cold empathy gap theory 13–14
Hume, D. 54n7
Humean subject 74, 80, **87**

ICs 2–4, 8–11, 45
IC theories of the perceived future self 9, 12, 20
identity: crisis 75; metaphysical 46, 48, 74, 82; personal 42, 46; practical (*see* agent)
imprudence 42–3, 45
indeterminacy of the future self 52
integrity view 102
interagential decision 49–51
intertemporal choices *see* ICs
intertemporal theories of the perceived future self *see* IC theories of the perceived future self

Jaworska, A. 97–100

Kant, I. 2, 38, 40–1, 72, 74
Korsgaard, C. M. 46–7, 50, 115
Kuczewski, M. G. 101–2
Kuhse, H. 102–3

later individual 106–8
liberalism 2, 41
Liberman, N. 17–19
Locke, J. 101

Margo 99, 101, 107–8
McKerlie, D. 78–9, **86**
mental construal 17–18, *21*
mentalizing *see* ToM
mental simulation *see* simulation
mental time travel to the future *see* episodic future thinking
minimax regret principle 77, **86**
morality: other-regarding 2; self-regarding 2, 46, 50

moral risk aversion 44, 77
Moral Theory of Prudence 61–74

Newton, M. J. 102
nineteenth-century Russian nobleman 94–6
nonidentity problem 71–2
normative principles of actions 47–8
Nussbaum, M. C. 64

objective ignorance 52
obligation to preserve the future self's agency 62–5, 69–70, 72
O'Connell, G. 14–17, 23
open present *see* right to an open present
original position: intrapersonal 75–8; prudential (*see* intrapersonal original position)
overarching IC theory of the perceived future self 2, 8, 22–3
overarching intertemporal-choice theory of the perceived future self *see* overarching IC theory of the perceived future self

Parfit, D. 12, 42–3, 45, 51, 74, 80–1, **87**, 95–6, 100
perceived similarity 12, 19–20, 24
perception of the future self 10–12
Persad, G. 102–3
person: identity of (*see* personal identity); metaphysical 46, 48, 74, 105
personal identity problem *see* problem, of personal identity
personhood 102–3
perspective: imagine-other 23–5; imagine-self 23–5; taking 11, 23–4, 26
Pettigrew, R. 81–3, **87**
planning ability 47
positive response 79, **86**
practical agent *see* agent
practical identity *see* agent
practical reasoning 40
practical wisdom 41
present-self–future-self relationship 50–3
primary goods 64
problem: of personal identity 94, 99–106; of possible future selves 77, **86**

prudence: ancient view of 40–1; modern view of 40–2; and morality 40; morality of 40–5, 69
prudential goods 83
psychological connectedness 28n7, 42–3
psychological continuity 12–13, 19, 22–3, 42–3, 80, 100, 102–3, 105
psychological distance 17–19
psychological similarity 105–6

Quante, M. 108

rationality: objective 76–9, **86**; of prudence 43; prudential 83; requirements of 40–1; subjective 77, 79
Rawls, J. 64, 75
reasons: for action 4, 47; objective 79–80, **86**; subjective 76, 79–80
regret 44, 50, 77–8, **86**
relation R 43, 80, **87**, 88, 100–1
responsibility: backward-looking self-regarding 67–8, 73; forward-looking self-regarding 61, 67–8, 73–4; moral 52, 67
right to an open present 65–7
Robertson, J. A. 101, 105

sacrifice 41, 45, 82–3, 85, **87**
Schmidtz, D. 116
Schofield, P. 72
self: changing 81; *see also* agent
self-control 13, 18, 25–6

self-projection 11–12
self-regarding veto power 51, 96
Sidgwick, H. 41
simulation 14
simulation accuracy 14–15
simulation efficacy 14–15, 17
simulation model of intertemporal preferences 14–17
Smith, A. 42, 59
stereotyping 17, 21–2
Strawson, G. 45
strong causal relation 52–3, 68, 105
suicide 66

temporal neutrality 41, 44
temporo-parietal junction 15–16
theory of mind *see* ToM
ToM 11–12
Tomlin, P. 88n8
transcranial magnetic stimulation 16
transformative experiences 48–9
Trope, Y. 17–19

utility 44, 76–7, 81–3, 85, **86–7**

veil of ignorance 75
ventromedial prefrontal cortex 11
Vitrano, C. 105–6

weakness: of imagination 25–6; of will 25–6
well-being 2–3, 38, 41–2, 45, 73, 79, 83, 85, **86**
Williams, B. 77

For Product Safety Concerns and Information please contact our EU representative GPSR@taylorandfrancis.com
Taylor & Francis Verlag GmbH, Kaufingerstraße 24, 80331 München, Germany

www.ingramcontent.com/pod-product-compliance
Lightning Source LLC
Chambersburg PA
CBHW052101230426
43662CB00036B/1733